LIVING THROUGH TRANSITIONS

Harnessing your courage at a personal crossroads

Dr. Sharyn Salsberg Ezrin
Psychologist

Updated Second Edition

"This is an inspiring book that has a holistic approach to life transitions. Through her personal and professional experience, Dr. Salsberg Ezrin brings a distinct wisdom to the entire process, respecting the impact on our well-being and our relationships, and focusing on the importance of self-awareness. The stories provide us with reassurance and hope that one can emerge from life's most difficult times with a renewed sense of spirit and courage. There are wonderful lessons to be learned from reading this."

— DR. JENNIFER BAYANI, D.C., DIPL. ACUP.,
Chiropractor and Acupuncturist

"Based on her extensive experience, both professional and personal, Salsberg Ezrin shares her insights on some of the voluntary and involuntary transitions that could be facing us all. This book raises issues that should be discussed widely."

— MARGRET HOVANEC PH.D., C. PSYCH., Psychologist,
Toronto, Canada

"In executive search, I meet many people grappling with a professional transition. Their journey will greatly benefit from this book, helping them develop courage of the heart in dealing with the unexpected, and courage of the mind in pursuing their plan. Dr. Salsberg Ezrin becomes their personal career coach, offering key action points backed by worksheets and rich stories of lived experiences, which include her own."

— ANDREW J. MACDOUGALL, elected member,
worldwide board of directors, Spencer Stuart

ISBN: 978-1-4120-6840-6 (sc)

Trafford rev. 04/26/2019

North America & international
toll-free: 1 888 232 4444 (USA & Canada)
fax: 812 355 4082

DEDICATION

My labour of love in writing this book is dedicated to our daughters, Rachel and Shaina. I admire your courage as you both learn to manage your own transitions as challenges and opportunities.

Hershell, you have been my partner in this new adventure of writing, rewriting, rethinking and clarifying all that I wanted and needed to say. Our lives together have been a remarkable series of transitions. May we continue to share the joy and courage it takes to reinvent and recharge how we live and love and make the world a better place.

TABLE OF CONTENTS

PREFACE TO THE SECOND EDITION

My decision to proceed with a second edition of this book, almost two years following the release of *Living Through Transitions*, came after my father, Nathan Salsberg, passed away, on May 27, 2007. This edition is my way of honouring my father, and his determination to live life to the fullest, whatever obstacles or problems came his way. He was a great role model for my early transitions as I searched for opportunities to fulfill my own dreams. I wanted to salute his courage and striving for solutions until the end.

As I recalled Dad's shift from living independently to accepting his increasing physical limitations, I realized how, during his lifetime, he had helped his children and grandchildren to become more fully aware of the values he cherished.

Some memories of Dad's last year stand out for me. For example, he found he could no longer dial his family's telephone numbers because of his arthritic fingers. He was thrilled when we solved the problem by getting him a telephone with large buttons pre-programmed to reach us, each button lined up next to our pictures.

Dad, who was a custom tailor by profession, decided he did not want to keep some special suits and jackets from his wardrobe. But before offering them to members of the family, he told us what events he had made them for; he remembered every suit he'd made for himself and why he had made it.

Dad had always enjoyed meeting new people and sharing stories during the years he ran his business. His customers became very loyal, not only as suit-buyers but also as friends. When Dad became older and more infirm, I asked him to talk to social workers about his increasing frustration and sense of isolation and he agreed. The social workers listened attentively to his life stories and by doing this, gave him the

gift of acknowledging that he had led a very interesting and fulfilling life. During some talks with them, he told stories he had not shared with his family before. He described his memories in vivid — and joyful — detail. He relished telling these tales because he loved to see people's reactions, especially his family's. Frequently, my husband and I were there when Dad talked about his life and history, so we were able to hear his important memories and share in his recollections.

As Dad's condition declined, he welcomed our invitations to take him and Mom out for a meal, a movie or even just window-shopping to see what was in fashion in clothing shops. He glowed from the special attention we paid on his birthday every October 30. February 2007 was especially memorable because Mom and Dad celebrated their 60th wedding anniversary with a toast of champagne to each other and their special marital partnership.

However, as he became increasingly infirm, each occasion felt like it was the last. During what turned out to be his final year, his determination did not flag, even though he became progressively more frail. Dad always faced his problems with creative and single-minded determination. At one point, a social worker arranged a place for him in a twice-weekly activity program for seniors. He enjoyed it for a few months, but eventually, he was no longer able to participate.

It was his increasing inability to figure things out that caused him the most distress. He gradually became incapable of reasoning through a problem. What comforted him the most was sharing whatever he had on his mind. I listened to what he wanted to say, but it was very difficult. I loved and respected my father, but my empathetic feelings sometimes made me feel I was drowning with him in his loss of control. I was grateful to hear his thoughts, even though some of them were terribly hard for me to hear. Dad saw his life coming to an end, and he was philosophical in an attempt to comfort

me. My true grieving began at this point, before he died. He was trying hard to help me be prepared, but of course, I did not want his life to end.

However, our shared experience—the fact that I was intimately involved in his last years—brought a deep calm to me when he died, even though a part of me died with him.

ACKNOWLEDGEMENTS – SECOND EDITION

This second edition provides me an opportunity to thank the people and organizations who supported Mom and Dad during their renewed life in assisted-living. Since September 2002, and their move to Forest Hill Place, Mom and Dad returned to a residential neighbourhood they loved and had left in the early 1980's. They bought their first home nearby when parts of Toronto north of Eglinton were covered in farmland. Mom and Dad purchased our newly built family home after I was born in 1948. I lived there for 22 years until I was married.

Dad charmed the staff at Forest Hill Place with his personal style. He truly appreciated all the support Mom was receiving as she adjusted to her life after her stroke. In their first years there, Dad pushed Mom in her wheelchair to activities and meals. Their routines were very similar, and yet they each found ways, with the compassionate and personal support of the staff, to continue to have time for their own privacy. I am grateful to everyone at Forest Hill Place who have nurtured and supported Mom and Dad over these past 5 years, and continue to enrich Mom's life.

I would also like to thank Pat Irwin who, through her personal service business called ElderCareCanada, helped to facilitate and co-ordinate many changes we made for Dad as he continued to need extra support services. Pat has been a remarkably creative and steady guide to our family, and a uniquely caring friend to me through my transitions.

The social workers and medical team from Baycrest supported Dad in an exceptionally professional and understanding way. I want to thank everyone who assisted Dad cope with his despair and frustration. Finally, I would like to express my gratitude to the caregivers from

HomeStead CareProviders. Each one came with their hearts open to Mom and Dad, and made my life easier. I could not have managed to carry on without their daily support. My deepest appreciation to you all.

INTRODUCTION

Whenever a person's life unfolds in a new or unexpected way, we call that process of change a transition. The *Canadian Oxford Dictionary* defines transition as "1. a passing or change from one place, state, condition etc. to another".

In my 25 years as an organizational psychologist and, most recently, 12 years as an executive coach, I have helped many people plan and execute transitions in their careers. Most often, their reason for considering a change is that they want to alter or leave a situation or circumstance that no longer feels right. Together we consider how to remake their work life and renew their energy and sense of fulfillment. In my private practice, I have worked primarily with baby-boomers, assessing the next steps in their careers after they have worked for at least 20 years. Some decide to scale down their work commitments, others want to build a new work regime, but all need and want to keep generating income.

Not only do my clients want to earn, they also want to be the creators of their own work worlds. There are many ways of redesigning a work situation to make it different or less demanding. The process of looking back and assessing what has been, and then looking forward to find out where to go next, requires a holistic perspective. Once people reach their 50s, many of them come to want their work and home lives to be more interconnected. The redesign might require a very different type of work setting or a new work routine, as well as other elements that cannot necessarily be predicted at the start.

Other people may have had a transition thrust upon them, when they lost their job or suddenly had to care for an aged parent or went through a divorce. Very few self-help workbooks or career guides talk about unexpected life or

work transitions. Almost everyone who goes through such unplanned and disruptive events feels as if their life has been permanently changed.

How this book is different

There are many excellent books that take a step-by-step, self-directed approach to the experience of transitions. They include:

- Richard N. Bolles's *What Color is Your Parachute? A Practical Manual for Job-Hunters and Career-Changers*. This was first published in 1970. It is the most comprehensive career guide available, and is updated annually. It is aimed at people looking to begin what Bolles describes as a "Life-Changing Job Hunt."
- Paul Tieger and Barbara Barron-Tieger's *Do What You Are: Discover the Perfect Career for You Through the Secrets of Personality Type* (1995). This guides the reader's process based on the relationship between their personality type and career satisfaction.
- Marsha Sinetar's *Do What You Love, the Money Will Follow: Discovering Your Right Livelihood* (1987). This offers examples of how people made changes to their work lives that helped them rekindle their enthusiasm for earning and being fulfilled.
- Mary Lindley Burton and Richard Wedemeyer's *In Transition* (1991). This was developed as a career seminar for graduates of the Harvard Business School MBA program.

These books focus on making the transition period as efficient and productive as possible. A book can be a helpful beginning, in that it provides a structured plan for the reader to follow. However, it takes a lot of effort to reproduce a program. In addition, forcing yourself to follow a set program may undermine your experience of a personally meaningful transition. In other words, these books focus on using the process as a means to an end.

This book, on the other hand, emphasizes the experience of the transition as an end in itself.

I will be talking about:

- Two distinct categories of transition experiences: those that are unplanned and life-altering or planned and life-enhancing;
- Two distinct processes for unplanned and planned transitions; and
- The value of the transition journey as an opportunity to gain new emotional and psychological self-awareness.

Courage of the heart and courage of the mind

I believe we need a new lexicon for the way transitions are identified. If people's transitions are prompted by unplanned or unexpected events or circumstances, it is their heart that feels the impact first. Unplanned transitions, whether life- or work-related, usually have abrupt beginnings. When your transition begins unexpectedly, it is your heart that reacts. Your heart reveals how you truly feel. What helps you move beyond the initial shock, despair or sense of confusion is *courage of the heart*. Ultimately your heart becomes a source of hope and strength. We all show courage of the heart when we talk about how we feel and rediscover our own resilience.

When a transition involves choosing a new direction or setting new priorities in your work or personal life, you require *courage of the mind*. This means you need to develop a strategic plan that maps out the steps required to bring about the desired shift. Courage of the mind gives you the fortitude to stick to the path and brings you to the end of the transition feeling rejuvenated. Some of the individuals I interviewed for this book had specific expectations that provided a focus for their efforts. Others were simply moving away from a

situation they could no longer tolerate. Planned transitions can, therefore, be either proactive or exploratory.

Transition stories

This book provides you with stories from a number of transition experiences that may have themes similar to your own. In total, I heard 75 transition stories from men and women born between 1946 and 1964. Approximately two-thirds (47) talked about planned life and work transitions. The other third (28) told stories of their unplanned transitions. To preserve the confidentiality of the story-tellers, names and circumstances have been altered.

Hopefully, you will find some gems among this treasure trove of insights and personal understanding that reflect and illuminate your transition experience. Beyond learning from what others have been through, you may discover that your situation is less stressful and traumatic than some described here.

Why I wrote this book

I have often used the planned-transition process offered here over the course of my career and life. But the process for unplanned transitions I developed only recently, and is based on my life experience over the past five years.

I had a dramatic health-crisis transition in the fall of 2000. It was unlike any transition I had ever planned or faced unexpectedly because I did not know how or when it would end. My transition lasted three years, and my work and life situations have changed as a result. Finding new ways of living and working was key to my new understanding of unplanned transitions.

I decided to research stories of others who had experienced work or life transitions so I might test out some of the ideas and approaches I had developed for myself.

INTRODUCTION

It was after I had completed about 40 interviews that I knew I could make the idea for this book a reality. I had written and published articles in the popular media for years, but the prospect of moving from this to the serious effort of researching and writing a book was the start of a new work transition for me. It was planned, but I encountered many u-turns and unexpected obstacles that slowed my progress. Looking back over these past two years, I feel grateful for having had the time and opportunity to write a book, but consider this kind of time and mental commitment unrepeatable.

I want to share my experiences along the road with you. In this book, I have combined my perspective and experience with excerpts from the transition stories I heard. As you go through your own transition, I hope you will be able to benefit from the lessons of my experience and the experiences of the people I interviewed.

MY TRANSITION STORY

MY TRANSITION STORY

CHAPTER ONE

My life's work has been helping people to make planned transitions in their work lives. Many times throughout my own life, I too have had to make transitions to accommodate professional and family challenges.

Life: a constant flow of planned transitions

My life has been full of many planned and unplanned work and life transition experiences, many of which related to moving from one city to another.

Just for background, here is how my early married life unfolded. As the wife of a Canadian Foreign Service officer, I travelled with my husband a great deal, moving to a different city whenever he got posted. He worked in this role for almost 14 years. We lived in four cities in three countries and relocated five times, and each time, we encountered a huge learning curve.

Our experiences taught us some key lessons about life and work transitions. We gained some unique life skills: taking care of our personal and health needs first: finding doctors/dentists, babysitters, grocery stores, schools for our children and, finally, unpacking our personal effects. We also wanted to feel comfortable and safe under our new roof, with all our personal things around us.

What we learned is that no matter what you experience or how much you plan, you are never fully ready for these kinds of changes. However, as we went through the transition of each new posting, we learned we could build specific skills that suited us and got us through the process: how to find

good schools for our daughters, for example, or joining a faith community that was right for us. These tactics made successive transitions a little easier and a little less disruptive.

The biggest adjustment related to finding friends. We found the emotional and practical realities of separating from our family and friends in Canada or in other cities were a natural part of the transition to a new posting. We knew it was important to find ways to keep in touch with the people we left behind, and to build new support systems in our new location. One of the ways we did this was by inviting family members and friends to visit us and meet our new communities of friends wherever we were living.

Our cumulative experience in adjusting to new cities, new cultures and new responsibilities helped us, long after leaving the Foreign Service, to feel confident in facing different kinds of transitions. We weren't always excited and enthusiastic about the prospect, but knowing we each had been through other transitions, we knew we could turn to each other, or people we trusted, for the support we needed. In most cases, we made it through relatively well. We actually began to enjoy the surprises more and more, and they often enriched our experiences.

In fact, I have tried, since we lived in India, to preserve some remnant of the more spontaneous rhythm of daily life I experienced there. I allowed my own plans to merge with the unexpected along the way, and as a result, my transitions were fuller and more meaningful experiences. What I also found was that when the transition was over, I was able to sustain what came next.

However, when I was struck with a mysterious joint inflammation in the fall of 2000, I was faced with a kind of transition that was entirely new to me.

In reflecting back on my ability to meet this challenge, I quickly realized that a sabbatical taken in the summer of 1998 had influenced how I dealt with my health crisis.

Planned transition: my sabbatical

My three-and-a-half month sabbatical in the summer of 1998 was my first taste of living through moments in time without having a goal or an outcome in mind.

As I talked about it with clients and colleagues and began to arrange back-ups for clients during my absence, I discovered who would miss having access to me for this time period and what people valued about how I helped them. The preparation process also helped me understand what it takes to remove all work obligations, and how to phase out or reduce personal activities during the time away (such as my regular volunteer activities) so they could be started up again when the sabbatical was over.

One of the most important influences in my desire to try a time-out, as I thought of it, was my growing interest in the world of mindfulness meditation. I read a number of books and articles that year about learning to live in a mindful way, cultivating a condition of being rather than doing, and learning not to judge the thoughts and impressions that can clutter one's thinking.

Several key leaders of the mindfulness movement have influenced therapeutic techniques used with individuals experiencing chronic pain and cancer. The first book to have an impact on me was Jon Kabat-Zinn's *Full Catastrophe Living: Using the Wisdom of Your Body and Mind to Face Stress, Pain, and Illness* (1992). In this book, Kabat-Zinn, who has done pioneering work in the field of mind-body medicine, describes what prompted him to found the Stress Reduction Clinic at the University of Massachusetts Medical Center and what the program offers. Kabat-Zinn described *Full Catastrophe Living* as "a navigational chart, intended for people facing physical or emotional pain or reeling from the effects of too much stress."

A year after my sabbatical, I had the opportunity to

participate in a one-day workshop with Kabat-Zinn. He led the group through an entire day of mindfulness meditation. This experience cemented my acceptance of the value of bringing mindfulness into my daily life. It was serendipitous as well, because I did not know how soon I would be testing the principles of using the wisdom of the body and mind to heal.

Unplanned transition: my body rebelled

In the fall of 2000, I was struck with severe and continuous joint pain. I knew I needed more than just another sabbatical. Something was seriously wrong. I was experiencing swelling, intense heat and pain in most of my upper-body joints—neck, shoulders, wrists, hands—and knees as well. I realized I needed to re-evaluate how I had been living my life up until that point. In addition to a full schedule of work and personal pursuits, I was helping my parents through life transitions related to aging and declining health, plus going through menopause myself. Looking back, I can't help but wonder if this combination of stresses caused my body to react like a bridge buckling under a too-heavy load. Basically, my body said to me, "You can't go on living like this. Something has to change."

My first instinct was to look for something or someone that would help me discover what had triggered my condition and then find a way to prevent it from happening again. This was an automatic reaction, a pattern of problem-solving I had counted on and used professionally and personally for many years.

But I quickly realized that this time, it wasn't going to work. If you think about how we typically try to solve problems that have mysterious origins, often we get stuck. This is because the problem-solving approach works best when you can reasonably predict the results of your actions. My goal

was to become pain-free, but since I did not know what was wrong with me, I did not know what to do to make the pain go away.

I also had to consider the possibility that I might not be *able* to make it go away. This was a defining moment in the healing process. I realized that knowing *why* this had happened would not help me with my daily difficulties. I was in constant pain, severe enough that it was interfering with my sleep, and for a long time I could not even open a jam jar or hold a large mug without assistance.

This led me to a significantly different path from any I had taken before. I started reaching out to people who knew me very well and whom I trusted to guide me towards a healing process.

The process of rebuilding

The first person I turned to was my yoga teacher. I had been involved with Yoga Centre Toronto, a community yoga centre, for 10 years. When the pain began, I had just finished a week-long yoga workshop, so I went to Marlene, the centre's director, and said to her, "Look what's happened to me! I can't do anything. Everywhere I'm in pain." She, too, was mystified by my condition, but suggested I stop the weekly yoga practice I had been doing for several years and switch to an individualized special-needs class so she could see what had changed and could adapt my practice to support loosening and healing of the joints. I felt complete confidence in Marlene as she took me under her wing and introduced some very calming and strengthening poses that I was encouraged to practice daily at home. This was my first experience of allowing others to take over and guide me through a process, rather than directing the process myself.

This changed my entire focus from "Why did this happen?" and "What was going on in my life that caused this to

happen?" to believing the flare-up was a turning point and my life was about to be transformed. It was the start of a new way of assessing everything I was doing in terms of whether it was helping or hindering the healing process. As Marlene said, what was happening through my yoga was "a surrender to the opportunity to rebuild."

My newly altered yoga practice was what kept me afloat through the early days of pain. It helped me to face the many other changes I began to make. As soon as I felt some pain relief from yoga, I started non-vigorous swimming (for comfort rather than as an aerobic activity) several times a week, for at least 15 minutes at a time, and enjoyed the relief of pain as I floated in the water. I stopped sitting at my desk for long periods, and walked around to keep my joints flexible. I stopped aerobic activities like jogging and weight-bearing activities like strength training, which put an extra burden on my body and compromised the healing. This was difficult for me, because I had always been a very physically active person, but I had to listen to my body now and allow myself to rest.

My new routines as I explored new options

I also sought traditional medical attention right away. I went to my family doctor, who sent me for X-rays and to a rheumatologist. Both women had known me in long periods of good health, with occasional brief medical problems, and all of us were puzzled by this condition. I had never had any major health problems aside from psoriasis, a non-contagious chronic skin disease related to the immune system.

As we attempted to uncover the best approach to reducing the pain through medical means, I continued to seek other sources of relief. On my daughter's recommendation, I began to see a chiropractor who helped relieve the muscle stiffness with soft tissue therapy and acupuncture. I even convinced my husband to join me at a spa at the Dead Sea in Israel—I had

gone to this spa previously to treat my psoriasis—for a week of sea-mud treatments, which work as an anti-inflammatory. While I was there, they also suggested acupuncture for the pain, which yielded immediate short-term reductions in the swelling of my joints.

In March 2001, I finally had a diagnosis: psoriatic arthritis, a specific type of arthritis that develops in approximately 23 percent of people who have psoriasis. Like rheumatoid arthritis, psoriatic arthritis is an autoimmune disorder, though the effects are usually milder than rheumatoid arthritis. I was put on medication and finally began to feel a lessening of the pain and swelling. The months passed with increasing improvement, and within two years, the arthritis was in full remission.

However, I realized how powerful the medications were when I tore the rotator cuff in my right shoulder while playing golf and did not even realize it at the time! I started to wean myself off the many pills I was taking daily, and discovered how these medications had masked the symptoms. Naturally, I did not want to live in constant pain, so I searched for alternative therapies. They have become my staple, and the pain in my shoulder has eased. I know this vulnerability can limit my physical activities, but I am prepared to keep strengthening and stretching daily so that I avoid further injury. So far this is working.

How I am giving back to people who helped me

What made the transformation I experienced so meaningful for me was the fact that the changes I introduced into my life were not the only things that helped me to heal. The support many people gave me during my transition also contributed to gradually calming my body. For me, this was the constant throughout my transition: the value of so many new guides in my life who helped me to weather the crisis. Their

involvement was essential to my mental, emotional, physical and spiritual health. Some were people who were in my life before the transition, but I also made new acquaintances with people who brought new perspective and understanding. All have helped me rebuild and reinvent how I live and work with a new focus: living to support wellness. I am now living differently because of their guidance, and my willingness to listen and learn from them is a new element in my life.

My way of giving back is very concrete, beyond expressing my appreciation to them personally. My book will be my gift to all who have helped. I want them all to know how much their support has meant to me. They were key to my getting to where I am today. Unlike my life before the health crisis, I am now being more open and expressive of my gratitude as I live my new level of fullness each day.

What can the support of others during a transition or crossroads bring? If anyone had asked me that question before my arthritic flare-up, I would have probably had a pretty typical answer. They can tell me what steps to take and give me their objective or specialist view of what might help me. They can provide moral support and help me hope that I will get past it and move on.

I now realize this is a very one-dimensional point of view. It does not reveal the depth of these people's involvement as my transition unfolded. These people were guides, helping me navigate my transition. I would not have been able to do it without them. All were professionals in fields such as chiropractic and acupuncture and naturopathic medicine, which I had never used or needed before. I was much more open to experimenting with techniques to bring healing or relief, and that was very different for me. Alternative therapies help support the body's own ability to heal. I had never understood this before.

How I found meaning in my transition and began moving on

The process of redefining my work and personal life changed me as much as the disease itself, if not more. My physical appearance has altered—it is subtle, but people who haven't seen me in four years or longer will often say, "You look different. What's changed?" An important part of the transition process for me was accepting I would never be the same again and my life would not simply go back to the way it was, even when the arthritis went into remission. A life-altering transition is just that: a permanent change.

I was able to resume a full, relatively pain-free life because I changed how and what I was doing. That change was not mapped out before it started. As the days unfolded, I learned to live differently and work differently, to ensure the improvements I was making could be sustained over the long term. Gradually, I reduced my workload, my extracurricular activities and my circle of friends to a level that was comfortable for me in my altered state. I probably cut everything in my life back by at least half, if not more, of what it was before the arthritis developed. I am more selective now about the friends I have. I'm only interested in people who are supportive, for instance, because I no longer have the energy to be the only giver in a relationship. Friendships combining offering and receiving are ideal for me.

I also had to start telling people what was wrong with me, which was challenging at times. When someone as active as I had been starts to slow down, people notice. I sometimes found it difficult to talk about what had happened, because my condition is exotic enough that I would have to explain it in some detail. I also discovered some people do not react well to hearing about another's illness. They either avoid the subject completely or are not very understanding about the physical limitations. That was all part of my learning curve.

My body was clearly ready for a new way of living. I spent

the two years it took to heal finding out what that life was. My personal epiphany in all this was accepting this different life. It was probably the first time I had had no plan and no timetable. Fortunately, I had learned, from my sabbatical and my studies of mindfulness, how to allow each day to have value as the experience took shape. The whole process was a creative exploration with a very gradual learning curve, and was slow enough that I have been able to sustain it.

The metaphor that comes to mind for my transition experience is being dumped on a water ski run without a towrope to get me back up. My life preserver kept me afloat, but I was far from shore, so I had to wait for the boat to return and the crew to pull me out of the water, just as I had to allow the healing process to unfold when I could not rescue myself.

My book is my way of giving back. I am gaining a new sense of self-confidence and purpose from writing, and I hope these ideas and stories will be useful to others, too. The creative process of reflection and the sharing of ideas has been remarkable. It may be my only writing project with such a deep and personal message, but I will be sorry to have it end. The completion of the book is the point at which I move on from my transition.

MY TRANSITION STORY

CHAPTER TWO

After publishing *Living Through Transitions* in 2005, I gained a new perspective on my health-crisis transition through writing my book. I had spent five years creating a different work and personal-life balance after my arthritic flare-up in 2000. This period was a watershed in terms of altering my life priorities. My work life changed when I decided to participate only in programs or projects that allowed me to keep my new routines and live at a slower pace. It was the most difficult adjustment I have ever faced, because I was a typical career-focused woman of my generation.

My work identity had always mattered a great deal to me. I faced a major question: How could I rebuild my sense of who I am and what I do when my life had been so work-focused? Initially, I did not know how to answer this question.

I understood it far better when I decided to retire from my private practice as an organizational psychologist and executive coach as of June, 2007. With that decision I gave up the privilege of coaching people on career changes and how to confront and manage work-related challenges. My own answer to retiring from coaching and counselling: keep talking, thinking and writing. This is how Chapter Two of my own transition story unfolded.

My involvement in my parents' lives

My parents' new life routines, after my mother's stroke in April 2002, occurred while I was regaining my own mobility and strength. Chapter One of my transition story, "My Body Rebelled," began when I started to understand the cumulative

impact of being an accommodating and caring daughter over a 10-year period. Since the mid-1990s, my husband and I had helped my parents reorganize their financial affairs. We also helped them consolidate their living space when they moved from their townhouse into a new, one-floor apartment near our own home. Having them close by was hugely helpful to me, and it allowed them to live closer to family and accessible activities for all.

Mom and Dad's generation did not spend a lot of time thinking about their golden years, beyond wanting to live independently as long as possible. They did not plan for, or even want to consider, all the additional support they might need as they aged. One experienced social worker, whom I consulted about 10 years ago, told me that such scenarios are very common. Today's seniors, she said, commonly deny their lives are changing and that they will have to move from complete independence to needing help in their daily lives. Often, it's a crisis that suddenly shows families that their parents can no longer be self-sufficient.

This was exactly the scenario we abruptly faced. After my mother's stroke in April 2002 at the age of 84, she and my father had to move from independent living into an assisted-living residence because he could not care for her. As I facilitated and co-ordinated the change for them, I became the go-to person for new arrangements such as organizing the sale of their home, distributing, storing or relocating cherished personal effects. During Mom's hospital-based three-month stroke-rehabilitation program, I visited her almost daily. Her family all tried to boost her spirits as she came to terms with the impact of her stroke. But many new services and supports had to be added to help her and Dad live as fully as they could.

Meanwhile, I could no longer continue my earlier commitment to Mom and Dad in the context of my arthritic flare-up. I found it hard to find time because I was engaged in

making myself more healthy and able to function. It was very difficult for me to let go of my care-taking role. I had derived great satisfaction from giving back to my parents over the years, but this had also taken its toll on me, physically and emotionally. My decision to pull back from caring for them in a daily way didn't sit well with my image of myself as a devoted daughter, and my desire to support my parents. I wanted to return their support of me, not just when I was a child but also when my own daughters were growing up and they helped me enormously in terms of child care.

But I knew it was essential for me to pull back from caring for their needs as part of my attempt to return to a pain-free life. I found several key services for Mom and Dad to help them cope with their changing needs, but I could not assist them as regularly as I had done before.

For a few years after my mother's stroke, my parents' lives improved in their new set-up — and as a result, so did mine. They became involved in routines and activities at their residence, and this freed up my time for activities that helped me sustain and improve my health. We reached a new understanding in our relationship. I was no longer the only one who had the full picture of their needs and wants. I gave much of that over to the staff and support workers taking care of them. My brother also became more involved as a support. Mom and Dad gradually learned to accept and welcome the people who provided them with daily assistance.

I believe one of the big challenges facing baby-boomers today is figuring out how to plan our own life changes while at the same time accommodating the changing needs of our aging parents.

Spending time with my Dad in his final year

During his last year of life, my Dad became severely depressed because he could no longer look after himself. One morning

in August 2006, he called me after his breakfast. He said he did not want to go on living, but he worried about Mom. This was a totally different side to a man who had always told me, "Smile and the world smiles with you." He certainly had had difficult business setbacks, but he always seemed to be able to forge ahead with hope that he could and would resolve the problems.

Dad's morning telephone calls of despair — that call in August was the first of several — shocked me. I listened to him talk about how his life had become so empty as he increasingly lost his independence. He could not accept his physical limitations, and it was painful for him to realize he was unable take care not only of Mom but also of himself. Each time these calls came — and they were not every day — I called through to the residence to ask someone to check on him. That gave me time to drive over to be with him.

Dad's family physician, who came for scheduled appointments twice a week, had come to know Dad through his first four years in the assisted-living residence. One morning the doctor was conducting his round of appointments when Dad called me in distress. I told Dad I would come and arranged to meet him with the physician. At our meeting, the doctor recommended we ask a team from Baycrest, a well-known and highly regarded long-term-care facility and geriatric research centre, to assess Dad's overall physical and mental health. Over the next few weeks there were some good days and more difficult days as he waited to be assessed. He called me often and just wanted to talk. Mostly we spoke about what he was doing that day. He needed more structure and a sense of purpose. I offered suggestions. We talked some more.

This period of Dad's deep despair and personal frustration was emotionally draining for me. My own health was affected by Dad's emotional turmoil. I coped by booking more visits to my chiropractor to ease my aching and stiff joints,

as well as receiving acupuncture to relieve the pain. All of this seemed to help me stay ahead of another flare-up. One problem our family had to deal with was that my Mom and Dad had more disagreements during this period. As Dad needed additional support to prepare him for the day and for evening bathing, my mother felt she was being neglected by him. Unfortunately, he was not able to comfort her, only to reassure her that he was not less interested in being with her, he just needed to be by himself and rest.

The Baycrest Centre team who assessed Dad's mood and overall health prescribed an anti-depressant. They also suggested we encourage him to participate in a seniors' activity program offered there several days a week. Dad accepted the idea and I participated in several interviews with skilled and compassionate social workers to assess his suitability for the range of programs.

During these interviews I listened to Dad reflecting on the highlights and memorable moments of his life. The social workers associated with Baycrest's seniors' programs asked questions I had never asked Dad before, perhaps because comparative strangers were able to ask questions I, as his daughter, could not. He was thrilled by all the attention. The interviews seemed to put him at ease, and offered a window onto aspects of his life that had previously been unknown to me. Dad became an open book; he spoke freely in a way I had not heard in many years. Perhaps his despair was lessened somewhat by the experience of making his life understood and appreciated. His mood seemed to improve with all the attention and activity related to preparing him for his new routine. I watched him become calmer and more comfortable with all that he revealed. He was accepted into a Monday and Wednesday group at Baycrest for planned activities from 10 to about 2, including a hot lunch. During his involvement in the program he enjoyed the new routines. He welcomed the new support and the variety in his life, and he became more

upbeat and purposeful.

Six months later, he was admitted to hospital with heart failure. Just before midnight on a Sunday evening, two weeks after he had been admitted to hospital, we got a call at home from his private care-giver. She had been with him almost every day during his hospital stay and understood him well. She told us we should come to the hospital immediately.

It was a moment I will never forget. Her soft message: "Nat's pulse is very weak." We had seen my Dad that evening, and could not understand how he could be slipping away the day before he was to move to his chosen long-term-care facility. Dad died before my husband and I arrived. Dad looked very peaceful when we saw him. That helped me to realize he was ready; it is a lasting memory. We stayed with him until his body was taken to the funeral parlour we had pre-arranged. (Dad had already agreed to all the arrangements for his funeral). I am so glad we did not have to think about these details during our time with him but only had to emotionally come to terms with losing him.

Our family believes Dad planned this timing. We think he did not want to move to another home and disrupt Mom's life yet again. His transition to death, over a long year of declining health, with occasional spurts of energy and enthusiasm, was his way of saying good-bye authentically. He was a man of action, and when the action stopped, he knew it was the right time for him to go.

Since his death, I have thought a great deal about how I supported Dad through his final year. Having so much time together was, I feel, his wonderful parting gift to me. I cherish these memories as another chapter of my own transition story.

Learning to cope with my father's death

During the months after Dad's death, as I rewrote Chapter

Two of my transition story, I acquired a new perspective on life and death. All that I have experienced over the past year has made me more aware of what mortality means to me. I have lost many loved ones to serious illness and death before their 60s, as well as individuals whose public legacies have been formed over a long and meaningful life.

But there is nothing like losing a parent. I have spent a lot of time since my father died thinking about how much he influenced who I am and what I do. This has been part of my grieving process — and my learning process, my transition.

And as I watched Dad accept his own mortality, I realized I was a witness, not the driver. Being a witness reminded me of how it felt when I relinquished total control of his and my mother's daily needs a few years before. By the time Dad died, I had come to terms with my new role in my parents' lives. When I felt Dad was ready to let go, I reassured him that Mom would be all right. No one could replace his role in her life. He and I talked about how his encouragement and support had been key to her regaining her strength and confidence during the five years since her stroke.

My hope is to honour Dad's life in the context of realizing that I too had to accept a changing reality. So his departure is a turning point because it's a new beginning for all of us left behind.

PART ONE
COURAGE OF THE HEART

PART ONE

COURAGE OF THE HEART

Dealing with unplanned, life-altering transitions

What does the experience of an unplanned transition feel like? What happens to people who experience feelings of despair when what seems like their worst nightmare has come true? What can you do when your life seems to have turned upside-down and everything feels like it is beyond your control? In this part of the book, I outline five phases in the transition experience. You will find it useful to look at each in terms of five different types of activities that will help you deal with these inevitable moments in your life.

Phase I: **Accepting the emotional impact of an unexpected work or life event**

In my practice, and in the interviews I did for this book, I heard about a range of unexpected traumas that prompted personal transitions. In all of the interviews, their experiences—being fired, losing a loved one, getting divorced, caring for a suddenly aging parent—were seriously derailing.

When people try to make sense of what they should do at the start of a transition, they may feel hampered and

sometimes paralyzed by their fear of the unknown. They typically might ask:

- How could I have known this was going to happen?
- Why me?
- Why can't I just go back to the way things were before? (They may hope that things will somehow return to "normal" or even want to deny that anything has changed.)
- What can I do now?

Some people's fear and panic may also be expressed as sadness, anger, disgust or despair. Some of these feelings are directed at themselves, and some at the people or experiences that triggered the life-altering event.

For anyone facing an unplanned transition, the key to being ready to accept what has happened is to realize it is your heart that has been wounded. Unexpected transitions pierce the heart. To start the healing process, you must recognize that you need to get to know your heart better so you can help yourself heal.

Building courage of the heart: getting to know your emotions

How does courage of the heart differ from courage of the mind? The difference is, we have no easy way of understanding our heart on our own. Experiencing panic or distress is how the mind alerts you to the fact that something disturbing is happening to you. However, those emotions are prompted by your heart, and because of that, you cannot depend on your mind to explain what is happening. A common dilemma for individuals who try to understand what has happened to them and how to fix it is that they start by putting their mind in gear to analyze and interpret. Unfortunately, this may prove to be counterproductive. It may not be worthwhile to take time and effort at the start of a transition to try to make sense of what is going on. This type of analysis might be more useful once the transition is over.

In response to life's stressful circumstances, we may also show courage. This may come from confidence that we can do what we want or are expected to do. Once again, though, this confidence is rooted in the mind's ability to guide our actions, but it is our heart that has been hurt, so the patterns or situations from our past may no longer apply.

Confidence stemming from courage of the heart, on the other hand, comes in a very different form. Many call it faith in oneself. Faith in the way you can count on yourself can be described as hope. Although having faith in yourself while you are experiencing panic, fear, anger or despair is not a typical or natural reaction, developing faith in yourself will help you overcome your fear of the unknown.

Starting the healing process

There are no short-term solutions to healing your heart, but once you realize the heart, not the mind, is at the core of your feelings, the next step is to accept that you need help in repairing it.

Many of the people I talked to who experienced an unexpected change in their lives, whether it was a job loss, a business failure, illness or the loss of a loved one, were shocked and disoriented by the event. The feeling of being taken off guard is the mind's way of helping you understand you need to take a break. For some, the idea of giving themselves time to regroup helped them start fresh. Getting out of a discouraged or distraught frame of mind helped them to begin the healing.

Some people said, "I took the summer off." Some went on an overdue vacation or sabbatical. One of my interviewees saved a portion of his severance for a pre-planned family trip to Australia. They decided to take a longer trip, and enjoyed seeing old friends and being together as a family for several months.

Whatever precipitates the unplanned defining moment, it is helpful if you can see it as a gift to yourself. Usually, it is a gift of unplanned, uncommitted time. If you have some savings, then use as much of them as possible to do something for yourself or your family or friends. This break will help you get relief from the shock and the surprise of your transition. Giving back to yourself is healing for the heart.

At a time when the status quo of your life has been derailed and you feel wounded emotionally, you can also begin by asking these questions:

- Who can I talk to about how I feel?
- What can I do on a daily or weekly basis that will give me some relief from the despair I feel?
- How do I tell my transition story?

Talking about how you feel

Healing the heart requires the help of others. Anyone who has experienced the sudden shock of a work or personal upheaval has also experienced fear of the unknown. But if you want to bring your heart back to its state of emotional well-being and comfort, begin by surrendering to your fear and talking to people whom you trust. These people might have very different roles, from listeners to advisors to people giving you moral support and encouragement. Often, people you didn't know before the transition can become key supports during the period when you are charting a new course for your life. All these individuals will help you rebuild your daily routines and find ways to regain your feelings of confidence in yourself. Talking to them about how you are feeling—what you have lost, what you miss, whether you feel helpless or angry—will help clarify your experience and your emotions. As the novelist E.M. Forster said, "How do I know what I think until I see what I say?"

You may also discover the barriers that may be preventing

you from moving beyond the early period of your transition. In particular, listen to people who have faced such unplanned crossroads themselves. Each of them may have found that the experience affected them differently, but hearing them talk about it will help you understand what options you have.

Not only do you need to talk to people whom you trust but you also need to turn to people who can offer some guidance on what might help you begin the healing process. As you spend time understanding how to heal your heart—and to move through your transition as a healing experience—you will learn more about yourself. You will likely want to consider your options. How to go about exploring different possibilities is a very personal journey. You might ask for recommendations from people you know. You may also need the help of professional counsellors or therapists who will help you rebuild your confidence, perhaps people whom you have never known or worked with before. You will want to know if the new guides you find are people who can help you sustain the benefits of your transition.

Try to see this period as one that will open new possibilities for you.

Committing to daily or weekly activities

Part of discovering what your transition might include is deciding which of your activities or routines are important to you and which can be easily integrated into your transition routines. It is important to choose what you believe is sustainable even after the transition is over.

The people I interviewed gave many examples of activities they took up after they had experienced an unplanned transition. These included more intense physical workouts that made them feel both physically fit and calmer; learning how to meditate and doing it daily; taking weekly yoga classes and learning how to apply the benefits; finding new hobbies

such as painting; or doing a lot of walking or swimming as a way of relaxing and maintaining body fitness. These people also continued to do the things that always brought them pleasure, all of which helped to open their heart to themselves and others.

Telling your transition story

You are now beginning to understand that your transition experience has become part of a new "chapter" in your life. The early parts of this chapter probably contained warning signals that something was brewing. It can be worthwhile to try to remember some of the signs that things were about to change, so that any future transition can be anticipated. You don't need to be fully prepared for any future transition, and sometimes you simply can't be, but unplanned transitions are usually the most difficult at the beginning and are the most disruptive of your work and life routines.

All these elements—talking to others and building a network of guides, establishing routines and creating your transition story—will help you to find the best way for you to heal your heart.

The following list sums up the points made above. No matter how you use it, remember the experience of your life-altering transition will build a metaphorical foundation for handling any future such experiences. You will be better prepared to see the benefits and the disappointments, the bonuses and the compromises, for all future transitions.

Phase I: **Five ways to accept the emotional impact of an unexpected work or life event**

1. Talk to people whom you trust
   - What are the unknowns?
   - What do I no longer have?
   - What do I miss?

2. Commit to regular activities providing relief
   - What are the knowns?
   - What do I still have? What can I be sure of continuing to do?
   - What do I cherish? What will I do more?
3. Create your own transition story
   - When/what was the defining moment of my experience?
   - What were the signs/signals this was going to happen?
4. Find guides to help you navigate your transition
   - How do I find out how I am doing?
   - How do I check my physical, mental, and emotional health?
5. Learn about what you need to heal your heart
   - Whom can I talk to with experience of this kind of life-altering transition?
   - How have others moved beyond their transitions?

The lessons I learned over four years of transition

When I could look back from a place of far less pain, I asked myself what lessons I had learned and how I had changed the way I lived to allow the healing.

These are the daily commitments I made to myself:

1. Give yourself time: giving myself a very distant horizon for healing was very helpful when there was no clear path to follow.
2. Enjoy the journey with others: if your path can be shaped by involving others, your transition will become a personally meaningful journey.
3. Deepen relationships: the relationships you build on through your transition will bring a difference to your renewed life, hopefully for the better.
4. Welcome reciprocity: you should welcome anyone who becomes involved in helping you through your transition and, in turn, offer to help when they face one.
5. Remember the details of the changes: you will want to tell your story to others and explain what is important to you now—that is part of the healing.

Phase II: Getting the support you need to rebuild your confidence

After separation or divorce

Both Tom and Eric were catapulted into single parenthood unexpectedly through divorce. Their greatest loss was the company of someone to support them in their lives. As self-supporting men, their transitions required new sources of emotional and practical support.

Tom's wife walked out when their second child was six months old. He was fortunate to have his mother in the same city; she helped him parent his very young children. His mother's immediate commitment was a remarkable boost to recovering his own faith in himself. Within a year, he went back to school to retrain as a social worker. He found new relationships that helped him a lot during the uncertainty of his transition, and once he had established his new work and life routines, he became open to trying other new ways of working and living. He learned how important it is to be open to possibilities.

For his part, Eric's final legal separation from his wife was underway when he received a $250,000 Amex bill on a joint credit card and discovered his soon-to-be-former wife had gone on a spending spree. His divorce coincided with leaving a company where he and his wife had worked together. Since he suddenly had a huge debt to repay to Amex, he decided to establish a home-based business, which allowed him to keep his expenses as low as possible. His teenage daughter was very supportive of their simpler life circumstance.

Unfortunately, with all this pressure, as well as the comparative isolation of his new working life, Eric began to drink heavily. With the encouragement of friends, he signed on for an alcohol and drug-abuse rehab program for a month. He began to realize how important it was to let his emotions come out and be emotionally expressive. He also realized he does not like to work alone all day.

After his month away, he continued to attend a weekly men's discussion group, where he could talk about his emotional ups and downs honestly. This peer support group was key to Eric's rebuilding his confidence. Now, he says, he has a job in an office and is much happier. He is not only living his life, both at work and home, with a new sense of purpose but he also has deeper bonds in all his relationships.

After losing your job

No one is ever totally prepared for the discussion when you are told you no longer have your job. Most aspects of this are personally devastating. You are asked to return special entry passes, give back company cell phones, credit cards and keys. Often, you will find your computer entry codes changed before you get back to your desk, and management will ask you to leave as soon as possible and not linger in the office talking to your (now former) co-workers. Most terminated employees are asked to arrange an after-hours return visit to clean out their desks and remove personal property. Sometimes they are allowed to delete personal correspondence from their computers under supervision or to print copies of their e-mail or telephone directories stored in their desktop computers.

At these job-termination discussions, people are usually given formal end-of-employment letters requiring their signature and return by a certain date. The severance and time frame for the loss of benefits are explained in these documents.

Going through this kind of unexpected work transition can be traumatic. People often feel they have lost their dignity, personal pride and sense of self-worth, as well as a work-based community of friends. Future contacts with the people with whom they have worked will likely be more difficult. This very emotional start to their transition is usually a significant blow to their self-confidence.

Job loss might arrive in other scenarios. Sometimes a job is redefined with no clear expectations. For example, you may be asked to take on extra responsibilities for which you are not acknowledged. Or you may be asked to assume a totally different role in your organization. These shifts also involve transitions.

Peter's transition began when, out of the blue, his boss told him he was no longer needed as a sales rep for the auto-parts company where he had worked for four years. Instead, the boss said he was moving Peter to the accounts department. Peter interpreted the transfer as a dismissal. Confronted not only with a potential loss of face but also a move he felt would tarnish his reputation, Peter contemplated his next steps. When he met with trusted colleagues, their positive feedback about his capabilities reassured him. Many encouraged him to build an independent practice and offer his services to the people with whom he had worked over the years. After consulting lawyers and mentors outside his organization, he went back to his boss and negotiated his departure from a position of confidence and strength.

During my interviews, some of the unplanned work transitions people talked about were prompted by an experience of betrayal. These people had accepted unusual and difficult work responsibilities but their efforts went unrewarded or, worse yet, ended up in job loss.

Mary worked for a small travel agency. While the owner was away on holiday, Mary put in extra time to satisfy special client demands and pick up the slack caused by the owner's absence. But when the owner returned, he told Mary her services were no longer needed. Mary knew she had been betrayed. She considered hiring a lawyer to contest the owner's decision, but realized that fighting over this would use up all her severance on legal fees.

Betrayal is one of the most damaging human behaviours in a workplace. The emotional reaction to betrayal is a mix of anger and frustration, along with a desire for revenge.

After she had worked for another, larger travel agency for a year, Mary decided to strike out on her own with one of her colleagues. Slowly, her business began to grow, and she felt a personal sense of victory when she realized she was more ready to run her own business than she had thought. This felt like the revenge she had wanted.

Often, though, the sense of betrayal described by my interviewees was not perceived as a personal attack but occurred when events beyond their control backed them into a corner at work. This was often the catalyst for discouragement and, ultimately, leaving or being fired from a job.

When Julie joined a consulting firm as a human resource management specialist, her partners promised her a significant management role. However, when she criticized some internal policies and practices and suggested different ways of doing things, her comments were ignored. At that point, she started planning her way out. Since she did not want to sacrifice her reputation in the industry, she had to plan her exit discreetly and carefully. As a result, the transition took longer than she wanted and was quite stressful. She admits that now, she has more modest expectations for her new work life. She also believes her current work situation is a better fit for how she wants to live her life: spending more time with her husband and children and volunteering in her community.

Sometimes a job turns out to not be as advertised, which can also cause a feeling of betrayal.

Clare had spent a year as a volunteer on a municipal government board when she was asked to come on staff as head of the enterprise. She accepted, even though she knew it was a controversial position.

Her transition began as she assumed her new role. She soon realized she had not been given a full picture of the culture within the organization. One of her colleagues had warned her about some of the possible problems that would emerge, but Clare did not expect them to become as personal as they eventually did.

She went through a steep learning curve, and took time to try to get to know her colleagues and understand the challenges. She did not experience as much stress in the early period of her transition as she did later on because, as she said, she was "in the eye of the storm." In fact, she found the transition exciting and rewarding, though she did give up personal and family time.

Unfortunately, though, during her four years in the job, she was continually forced to deal with growing resistance from her senior staff, who did not want to follow some of her new practices and policies that challenged the status quo. She, on the other hand, believed the changes she was implementing would become her legacy, and she was proud of what she was accomplishing. But the publicity that resulted from this internal dispute further undermined her reputation as a leader, and her work situation was never the same. She is now self-employed in an entirely different way, working only with clients she chooses, and loving it.

Getting the support you need

How can someone who has been betrayed by people whom he or she trusted regain a sense of self-confidence? There are different kinds of support systems you can count on for help in your unexpected life or work obstacles:

1. Family and friends who will help you rebuild your courage of the heart by being compassionate and caring towards you.

2. People who will talk to you about their own unplanned transition experiences. In the early period of your transition, friends or colleagues may introduce you to people to hear about their unplanned transition experiences. It is important to learn about how others felt at the start of their own transition experiences, as well as the things they did early on that they found helpful.

3. People who can provide an impartial perspective on how your feelings are linked to your behaviour or actions,

such as professional counsellors and coaches. I like to refer to the new people you may call on during your transition as guides. In my own case, these guides helped me to navigate and rebuild my life during my transition. The key to benefiting from these guides' involvement is to allow yourself time to try what they advise. This is a continuing process of planning actions, taking time to try out these actions and assessing how they helped.

Family and friends

The people who offer to support you usually want to get involved in your situation. They bring their own perspective to what has happened. If you ask them for their support, then you are asking for their compassion and emotional support. This is the best way to begin.

Martin, who has a young family, is living with multiple sclerosis. Since he was diagnosed, he explains he is now living differently: "I treat life like an adventure or an emotional marathon—it teaches emotional and mental stamina."

Mel was diagnosed with leukemia early in his married life. For him and his wife, Stella, this defining moment is the point in time to which every other period is measured. Stella says, "That is how we mark time."

Martin and Mel are both self-employed entrepreneurs who could not fall back on a corporate or organizational support system. As a result, their families played a critical role as emotional and financial supports. Stella says she decided to "grab hold of the situation and provide the strength" through Mel's transition of lengthy chemotherapy treatments and a life-saving bone marrow transplant.

For his part, Martin tries to "fine-tune his life in terms of his marriage and fatherhood" during periods of physical strength. He became more involved in his son's sports activities, and changed his work routines to accommodate his wife Linda's work demands.

The experience of a transition can often bring true feelings of friends and family to the surface. Expect a few surprises. Don't be disappointed if people whom you had thought you could include in your inner circle of trusted family or friends don't deliver. You may discover some people may even avoid you.

One of the things I encourage my clients to think about when they are planning a transition is whom they can count on to be there for them to encourage and boost their spirits. They may also discover that some of the people they had hoped to lean on will actually disappear from their lives.

One helpful exercise is to make a list of people you know and put them into one of the following four categories: co-operative, dependent, independent and in conflict. This requires a fairly hard-headed look at your relatives and friends, but it also allows you to anticipate where your support may come from. As a coach, I discourage anyone from starting to plan a significant transition if they do not have a group of people in their life on which they can count.

The same goes for unplanned transitions. In fact, it may be even more important to call on people early in an unplanned transition to ask for help, since you will be dealing with unexpected and upsetting events. Sometimes this acts as the first critical reality check to find out if your friends or family are able to stand by you when times are difficult. A number of the transitionees told me about friends who were no longer interested in a friendship when the transition changed the relationship. It is sometimes hard to know in advance how some people will react, but the old expression "fair-weather friends" is a common experience at the start of some transitions.

Peter's support system was the key to being able to overcome his sense of loss and anger when he was demoted to accounts and then left his job. During the early phase of his transition, he spent more time with his wife and children. He welcomed their ideas

about how to rebuild his work life so it would be in better balance with their family life. He was buoyed by the guidance, support and enthusiasm of his own network of mentors and colleagues. Peter was offered a significant contract from his first client and soon after, built an enterprise with a partner who brought in complementary skills. In time, he began to find the new work routines made sense for many reasons, and allowed him to target the kinds of projects and clients he wanted.

Getting the support you need is essential to your emerging from the transition with more energy and enthusiasm about your prospects. Support from people you trust is the best treatment for a wounded heart. Your renewed energy will be based on renewed confidence in yourself, and your belief in how you can rebuild your future personal life and work life.

When Clare left her job, she began another transition, and benefited from a great deal of support and encouragement to rebuild her work life. One of her first personal projects was to make a booklet for her niece's 18th birthday, called What I Wish I Knew When I Was Eighteen. *She learned through this transition how her confidence in herself had been undermined by the work-related rivalries and disputes.*

Managing the stress and disruption after an unexpected work setback or trauma takes time. Some people used physical or body-healing activities to help theme cope. Julie spent much more time with her family, offering them support on their special projects. Mary spent time helping her husband in his business. In all cases, people who had initially needed support later experienced a surge in their self-confidence as they spent more time with family and friends.

In fact, the key to successfully starting new work, whether as an entrepreneur looking for business clients or as part of a team of colleagues, is being comfortable with what you have to offer and who you are. If you are responsive to the needs and interests of your new co-workers or clients, your first months on the job will feel comfortable and safe. If you feel

self-confident, others will welcome your input.

The best preparation for the learning curve and potential surprises in a new job is to build courage of the heart. Become open to sharing who you are with your new co-workers. Appearing self-aware and confident helps secure their loyalty from the start. Your professional skills are a given: when someone is hired, their abilities and work experience have been carefully scrutinized. But when people display openness and self-confidence, this will demonstrate their interest in building friendships with their co-workers.

Phase II of unplanned transitions allows you to rebuild your confidence in yourself and strengthen your sense of being part of a circle of trusted friends and family. Whenever you recall your transition, you might find your memories of the times you spent receiving support are your fondest.

People who have been through the same experience

The experience of shock and fear that immediately follow an unplanned work transition is most dramatic the first time it happens. If this is not your first experience of a life or work transition, then you may know whom you can count on to listen to your story. These people will be very supportive of your revealing your emotions.

When Maurice's small film-production company failed, he did not lose the support of his colleagues. These people were familiar with the up-and-down cycle of feast or famine in the entertainment and media business. They had been through it themselves, and could offer their own lessons while helping Maurice to begin again. Because Maurice's business was heavily based on personal contacts, he was able to ask for favours. And the people who helped him join some new projects welcomed him enthusiastically. He wanted to keep his hand in the creative parts of the business, which he loved. He took a few contracts on spec, and the energy and momentum helped to make him feel he could count on these

people during the rebuilding period of his transition.

Professional help

In my work, I also function as a bridge for people on the day they are fired. I have a meeting with them after they get their termination letter and talk to them, in confidence, about their next steps. Usually their former employer has provided a generous severance package that includes some career-transition counselling and coaching. When I meet with someone immediately after they have been fired, I am there for two reasons: to help them through the initial shock and subsequent emotional release, and to encourage them to participate in a job re-entry service or outplacement sponsored by their company.

The provision of company-sponsored outplacement as the cushion after a firing has become common since it was first introduced in the late 1970s and early 1980s in North America. No matter what a fired individual decides to do, he or she needs to get back to work eventually. Outplacement companies offer workshops and encourage the use of specific tactics or techniques to make the process of a job search more foolproof and successful.

Many people's outplacement experiences include participating in meetings or workshops with others who are also job-hunting. These discussions encourage sharing of strategies and leads on job opportunities. Sometimes these structured gatherings provide new support groups and networks for individuals who have not met people outside their own work setting. They are often an especially helpful experience for people who have lost their jobs for the first time.

Generally, however, outplacement activities focus on looking for a new job. There is little emphasis on how to make the most of the time between when they stopped working

and when they accepted a new job. Returning to work after an unexpected job loss, for whatever reason, takes more than a job re-entry strategy. Rebuilding self-confidence takes courage of the heart. Whenever the transition allows time for strengthening personal relationships with family and friends, this makes the recovery from the loss more meaningful. In reflecting on the ways you allow yourself to benefit from this phase, ask yourself these questions as you welcome the support from others.

Phase II: Five ways to accept what has happened and get the support you need to rebuild your confidence

1. Talk to people whom you trust
   - Who is there for me now, and who is not?
2. Commit to regular activities providing relief
   - Which activities give me a boost now?
3. Create your own transition story
   - How do I explain what I am doing now?
   - What do I call it?
   - What is this chapter in my life?
4. Find guides to help you navigate your transition
   - How do I rebuild my faith in myself?
   - How should I spend my free time?
5. Learn about what you need to heal your heart
   - What are the main barriers I am facing while moving through this transition?

Phase III: Building new routines as you explore new options

Finding the courage to build new routines comes from having time to experiment. Whenever life shifts, especially during unplanned transitions, you can begin to reassess the importance and value of many of the things you were doing before the defining moment or shift. You might find yourself

assessing your activities as you discuss your situation with trusted friends and family.

Returning to an activity you've always liked

June and Eddy found that the process of preparing for an international adoption was very time-consuming. This transition was like no other they had experienced. They attended workshops with other potential parents of adoptees and described the "multiple layers of approvals" that were essential for being accepted by the agency they were working with. In order to qualify, they had to reveal their financial circumstances and accept the additional financial commitments. There was a lot of paperwork. During this period, June rejoined the rowing club she had belonged to for years. Rowing had been part of her weekly routine, but had been swept away by the complexity of the adoption arrangements. Rowing with friends helped her relax and, at the same time, regain a sense of perspective and also helped her through her transition to motherhood.

Whatever your transition experience, there are going to be parts of your previous life and work routines you decide to keep. These may be routines that are a genuine expression of who you are and how you would like to be known. For example, was there a time in your life when you used to have a weekly workout that you no longer have time for? Now is the time to bring such activities back into your life.

After Glen's wife died of breast cancer, he realized he had a deep need for companionship. His married life, which was a special partnership, had ended too soon. Initially, though, he was not interested in having a social life. It was a full year after his wife's death before he began to return to activities he had enjoyed before marrying: ballroom dancing, fishing, working out and playing tennis.

Glen compared his choice of isolation to how his 20-year-old daughter had coped. She had set out on a summer vacation

with friends within a month after her mother's death. Glen acknowledged his own transition with his decision to take his wife's pictures off the living room wall, 14 months after her death. He had begun dating, and wanted to feel he was making a fresh start. When he explained how he felt after his transition, he was excited to discover he felt younger and fitter than ever before. Glen enjoyed the dating, but eventually found he could live alone and have a full work and personal life without a partner. He said, "I discovered I did not want to go back on the old program."

Picking and choosing your favorite activities

Perhaps your transition began with a significant cutback in some of your preferred activities. This phase of rebuilding will allow you to pick and choose your favorites, and to drop the ones that are no longer useful or meaningful to you. My own routines shifted after my unexpected arthritic flare-up. My weekend morning yoga classes had long been part of an established routine, and after I became ill, I started special yoga practices to bring back my flexibility and strength. These new routines were key to my rebuilding my confidence that I could sustain some physically challenging routines after the transition. However, I decided to continue a weekly yoga class based more on the teacher I wanted to work with than the time of week. Weekends were no longer the sacred times for yoga. My work week changed to accommodate these classes, which was a very liberating decision.

The other changes I made in my routine were taking on fewer regimented activities at work and doing less work-related travel. The decision to write this book created new routines as my way of giving back to my community. The interviewing was a particularly important part of this project. Hearing other people's transition stories allowed me to build insights and create this tool.

Find something totally new to you

Why not do new things for their own pleasure? One of the ways baby-boomers are recharging their energy is taking up the musical instruments they used to play in a high-school band or orchestra, an activity they might previously have considered frivolous or unproductive. Sometimes they even organize regular jam sessions or music-making evenings. Some are finding out about community choirs or singing groups. In fact, singing is one of my favourite activities and I continue to include it in my own routines. Every few years, I choose a different choir.

As you make your choices and decide when and how often you include activities or commitments, try to imagine how they will fit into your life and work situation. When you build new routines, you may discover it is difficult to be as spontaneous as you were before the transition. It takes time to create new routines and feel comfortable.

The ultimate test of any new routine is whether you feel it is helping you progress through your transition. Some routines can create new energy and hope. You will likely discover yourself looking forward to these activities. Your trusted supports may even comment on how much better you seem to be as you cope with your transition.

Susan gave up a busy and fulfilling private practice in medicine after recovering from breast cancer. She and her husband researched all the treatment options in North America and became role models for and resources on the experiences of cancer treatment and recovery. Susan's return to new work and life routines includes her realization she is "living with uncertainty." Although she is buoyed by her success at demonstrating to herself she had the inner strength to get through the treatment, she feels the weight of her uncertain health status and has decided to live her life differently, "in the best way I can." She now spends any extra time she has supporting her children in their activities and has become a more

involved parent. She has a job she does not take home with her, and her working hours are flexible. She admitted the key change in her daily routines was creating a more balanced home and work lifestyle.

The chance to build new routines can feel liberating. Part of the benefit of taking time during your transition is that you might discover there are new things you would like to do.

In many ways, it was liberating for Michael to hand over the company he had created and nurtured. He had reached an unexpected financial impasse and knew the organization could not continue on its own. Handing over key staff and assets to the new owner was the defining moment that started his transition. At first, he felt a sense of loss and personal defeat, but this was also coupled with a newfound sense of freedom. During his transition, Michael took time to reflect on his effort to build a company. He gained new perspective on how the previous two years had compromised him. He came to realize he could now speak out on issues that really mattered to him. He became more open and uncompromising with people—key financial supporters in his company—whom he used to need to please. This new routine of speaking his mind was a big boost to his self-confidence.

Michael's first new commitment to himself was to make time to become more computer- and Internet-savvy. Previously he had counted on others to do computer-related tasks for him. After a short time, he realized these new computer-based skills were easier to learn than he had expected. He became comfortable and proficient in writing and developing presentations using his new skills.

Being brave enough to try new and different routines will allow your heart to feel hopeful.

Sandra returned from a business trip to find her long-term partner had ended their relationship, putting some clothes she had kept at his place in her bathtub and leaving a voicemail message with the news. Sandra had been an accomplished tri-athlete, and the day she discovered her partner gone, she decided

to sign up for an Iron Man competition. She completed it for the first time almost a year later, a day before her 50th birthday, and was thrilled with this birthday gift to herself. She has since completed another Iron Man and has attained a much greater level of proficiency and excellence.

The experience of new possibilities is very healing as you rebuild your confidence in yourself. This kind of confidence does not necessarily come from actual accomplishment or progress on new tasks or activities. Rather, the feeling of doing new things that you enjoy recharges your energy and enthusiasm for life. These are the building blocks of a successful and meaningful transition.

As you benefit from this phase of building new routines, you will want to ask yourself questions about the process of your transition. As you rebuild your routines, these questions will help you discover how you are progressing.

Phase III: Five ways to build new routines as you explore new options

1. Talk to people whom you trust and build a support system
   - Who can I count on to give me feedback on my progress?
   - How do I ask for feedback?
2. Commit to regular activities providing relief
   - How do I build these activities into my life?
   - What can I be sure of continuing to do?
3. Create your own transition story
   - How do I explain the benefits from these new routines?
4. Find guides to help you navigate your transition
   - Which routines will support my moving beyond this transition?
5. Learn about what you need to heal your heart
   - How will I know when I am ready to move beyond this transition?

Phase IV: Giving back to people who have helped you

Early on in your transition, you will have spent a lot of time with people you trust while you are rebuilding your courage of the heart. You may have talked to them about your situation and how you were feeling. Sometimes, though, accepting help can be difficult.

Several years ago, Judy was diagnosed with breast cancer. This was especially distressing since her mother had died from the same disease when Judy was 14. Judy visited a surgeon for a consultation and discovered he had been the one who had operated on her mother. That day, when she recalled what her mother had gone through, she says, "I fell on the floor and all I could think of was death."

At first she found it difficult to accept offers of help from her friends, family and support system because she had always assumed the role of helper and organizer. Eventually, she learned how to shift her attitude to welcoming what others gave to her, to the point that now, her transition story is full of gratitude for everyone who helped her through the period of treatment, surgery and regaining her strength. She explains her transition experience allowed her to learn how to "value the acts of kindness" she received from others. Judy is currently in remission, and giving time and help to co-workers who are facing their own cancer treatments and reaching out to people who are coping with chemotherapy and other cancer treatments. In Judy's view, the people who helped her have enriched her life, and she wants to do the same for others.

I heard many stories about the challenges of taking care of and supporting aging and frail parents, which is a transition not only for the parent but for the adult child as well.

Jane's transition began when she became the main guardian and caretaker after her mother's stroke. Because her mother lived alone and had been completely self-sufficient prior to the stroke, Jane had to make all the arrangements to change everything in her mother's life. One of the most important things Jane learned, and which she says has led to significant personal growth, is how to ask for and then depend on others to help. First, she had to give up her view of her

mother as a parent and support, and then she had to realize that she herself could not support her mother alone. She now draws on many new people in her life, and feels good about knowing they will be there for her and her mother when she needs their help.

As your transition progresses and comes to an end, you may want to offer to help other people with something they are facing as a form of reciprocity. Having the opportunity to show your appreciation is an important way to sustain your own healing. Building deeper and more valued relationships is key. These shared experiences will create cherished memories and strengthen the bonds of friendship. Building courage of the heart through giving back to others can also improve your feelings of confidence in yourself.

You likely have various relationships not only in your personal life but in your work-related communities as well. Sometimes, volunteering to help involves swallowing your pride—you may feel that as a result of what happened to you, other people will not respect you as they once did, which can be disturbing to your sense of self. This is particularly common if you have been fired from your job. However, try to tell your transition story with a positive spin on your next steps. As you rebuild your work life, you can also offer to do pro bono or volunteer work in the community during any extra time you have.

Demonstrating you have faith in yourself is best done through activities in which you give of yourself. When you offer to help others, your goodwill, energy and support will also nurture the courage of your heart. Ultimately, this gives you the strength to move forward beyond this transition.

Stories of people overcoming what initially appear to be insurmountable odds have a similar pattern to stories where a beloved family member or spouse has died. When you lose a loved one, the transition is clearly defined at the moment of the death.

Marcia's transition story began with the death of her father.

Before her father died, and with his guidance, she had developed a business idea, which had emerged from her discovery that there was no co-ordination among support services for elderly people who were frail and ill. Marcia ended up having to do it all herself. She now runs a small business that oversees and manages the move from a family home, the identification of special palliative or daily-living care needs, as well as nursing-home or retirement-home placements. Marcia recently added an extra service: helping with the disposition of property and family possessions.

Marcia took as much time as she needed to prepare to enter this brand-new area, and benefited from the support of her friends and family while she dedicated months to prepare and research her chosen field. She is thrilled with her new work life, and has moved on with a profound sense of how lucky she is to be able to combine what she is fascinated by mentally and creatively with a way of living and working. In effect, she is giving back to her clients and colleagues every day.

As you start to give back to people and feel the progress in your transition, you will likely be more confident about what comes next. You may also begin to be called upon by others facing transitions like yours who will ask you for advice.

As you grow into your new routines, here are some questions that will prompt you to consider how you might reciprocate to people whose support meant so much to your transition.

Phase IV: Five ways to start giving back to people who have helped you

1. Talk to people whom you trust
    • How do I reciprocate to the people who have helped me?
2. Commit to regular activities providing relief
    • How do I give back to myself and to others?
    • How can I be better prepared for the next transition?
3. Create your own transition story

- How have I benefited from this transition?
- What have I compromised through the transition?
4. Find guides to help you navigate your transition
    - Who will help me sustain my healed heart?
5. Learn about what you need to heal your heart
    - What lessons did I learn that can help guide what I do next?

Phase V: Finding meaning in your transition and moving on

Numerous people told me they were glad they went through a transition. Even though the event or circumstance that brought it on was difficult for them, they believe it worked out for the best. These individuals felt lucky that such circumstances had forced them to take a look at their work or their life in a new way.

When luck is part of the way someone describes their transition, it is the same as saying, "I am glad this happened to me." Many also called it a "wake-up call" when they referred to how the transition affected them. This was applied to a range of circumstances, including unexpected personal loss, a health crisis, a work or job detour, or even a tough conversation. Each forced them to look at their situation in a direct and honest way.

When people say they feel lucky to have emerged stronger and knowing what really matters to them, they bring personal meaning to their transition story.

For several years, James worked in Hong Kong for a Canadian company, managing its office there. An unexpected turn of events forced the company to close of all its offices in Taiwan, and James was assigned this task. After completing the closures, the company wanted him to return to Canada, but both James and his wife felt drawn to staying in Hong Kong. James realized he had to find work in a completely different field after a 20-year career of increasing responsibility. He took time to explore many options and obtained advice from people whom he trusted. There were many days of despair and pessimism, but the support he had from friends and former clients sustained him.

James's memory of a profound discussion with his grandfather helped to guide his thinking at the start of his transition. In the early days of James's career, he lost his first real job through downsizing. At that time, his grandfather spoke philosophically and forcefully about how to accept defeat, encouraging James not to take it to heart but to accept the turn of events and learn from them. James recalled his saying, "What doesn't kill you will make you stronger." James was able to use his transition to explore new ways of working with the skills and experience he had acquired in Hong Kong. Luckily, he made great strides in building a new and successful career. He has never looked back.

Typically, people in North America do not count on luck to guide their life or work. But in subtle ways, we all do hope for it and label unexpected events that turn out positively as having been lucky. The experience of having things work out well often brings a need to express appreciation. One way is reminding ourselves that we should not give up our hard-won courage of the heart.

Cindy's marriage broke up when, after her son, Graham, was born, she realized she could no longer stay in a difficult marriage. She spent the next decade as a single parent rebuilding her life with her son. Cindy basically gave up on finding another partner, but when she was finally ready to take more time for herself, her transition began.

It started when she was introduced to someone at a dinner party and subsequently became interested in him as a life partner. Cindy met her new partner at a time when she least expected it, and the transition was a great boost to her sense of confidence in life's meaning and possibilities. It also changed her outlook on life in terms of what she can do, both in her work and personal life. She told me, "I believe in fate, and I am not a religious person. I know I am a good person, and I have been seriously tossed around. I thought that eventually, with a good attitude, I could start propelling things in a positive direction." Cindy called her transition "lucky in life."

One of the main reasons these people's transitions turned out well was because they learned key lessons that influenced how they lived in the future. Many now have a perspective on life that helps them see things in a positive way—in other words, seeing the glass as half full as opposed to half empty. Whether the transition was work-related or personal, the experience went far beyond the realm in which it started.

Sylvia had tried to work as a salesperson in the competitive real-estate field. It was a significant departure from her earlier work life as an artist, and she quickly realized she had made a mistake. She did a lot of soul-searching to plan for her next job, and an honest and direct conversation she had with a friend helped her decide to get retrained in a field she had only known as a personal, creative pursuit and to become an art therapist.

Sylvia's transition brought rewards she had not expected. She was able to rebuild her work life, and feels hopeful she is now using her talents to the fullest. The wisdom she gained about herself from a lengthy transition has already shown benefits in her own artistic expression. One of the biggest things she learned was that, "You can't deny who you are. You have to lasso that energy and figure out how to make it work better."

Other transitionees found new meaning in their work lives as a result of their profound need for time to recover from the crossroads they faced at the start of their transitions.

Larry was unexpectedly fired from a job and decided to use his transition to get back to a life spent outdoors in nature, which had been how he started his career. He spent the summer and fall doing landscape gardening, enjoying the physical demands and seeing the results of his labours. He knew he could not do this for a long time, but he said it was an important first step, since it reminded him of how much being outdoors mattered to him.

In the past, Larry had worked as a ski patrol and later as a ski instructor outside Canada. During his first winter of transition, he worked again as a ski instructor. He considered a future in growing and developing a year-round resort company, but

PART ONE

unfortunately, there were no suitable work opportunities for him. However, these jobs helped him rebuild his confidence in himself, and brought him to a high level of fitness he had enjoyed many years before. He described how much the transition meant to him when he said, "You return to the good things about yourself, and things you like about yourself."

Sometimes, the support of a professional career and life coach is a necessary first step to rebuilding a career. Whenever people are forced from a job because of individual conflict or irresolvable disagreements, the impact on their self-confidence is devastating. A transition frequently offers the chance to redefine your work priorities and expectations for a sustainable and meaningful career and personal life. The resulting sense of renewal is a remarkable by-product.

Diana's work-related crossroad, after she was fired from a private foundation, left her feeling her reputation had been undermined. She was offered, and accepted, individualized assessment and coaching to help her reorient her career. This opportunity helped her gain a new understanding of the kind of work setting that suited her best, and she became equipped to make choices. Diana explained how her transition helped her move on to a job she believes is a much better fit for her work and life priorities. She also says she learned through her transition to face "my own demons and insecurities." In her new workplace, Diana is valued for all her talent and wisdom of years in the fundraising and not-for-profit sector. This was not how she was treated previously. She will never again undervalue her skills or personal creative talents.

Courage to find meaning in your transition comes from a sense of renewed confidence in yourself. It also comes from feelings that what happened to you brought more positives than negatives to your life. Most of the people I interviewed felt energized by the many benefits they experienced and chose to live their lives differently after the transition.

Some people used this opportunity to reconsider how they

would like to change their lives in profound ways.

Matthew had obtained a degree in industrial design and went to work for a small firm. Ten years later, the company went bankrupt. Matthew had become somewhat bored with his job, so he decided to take this opportunity to move into a different role and industry. He explained the start of his transition by saying, "It is important to get off the mat when you are knocked down." He was able to take some time to figure out what kind of work he could stay with and begin to build a very different career from the one he had left. He became a furniture-maker, which required him to go through a steep learning curve, but after the first six months, he already knew how well he had chosen.

You can combine your renewed courage of your heart with courage of your mind to give yourself a fresh start. Your mind will help you imagine a range of possibilities. You might even have a specific long-hoped-for dream that you never had a chance to test out. Why not let yourself consider a broad range of choices?

You can share your ideas and choices with the people who have helped you and supported you through your transition. If you feel bold and more courageous than you have ever felt, I recommend you try out these ideas and get feedback from people who know you well. If your unplanned transition gave you time to understand your heart's desires, you will not forget them easily.

Many people understandably feel hampered by a lack of savings or financial prospects at the start of their unplanned transitions. However, some of their bold new ideas did not bring any permanent financial hardships. Some took brief contracts to test out a certain field and see whether a change was what they really needed. This kind of experimentation is a sign of renewed hope. Others shifted their focus to activities that were aligned with specific passions or causes.

Many people who experienced difficult, unplanned transitions were prompted to question what they had been

doing before the transition. They used their last step to demonstrate to themselves they were no longer vulnerable to being caught unprepared again.

Here are some questions to make the concluding period of your transition a hopeful one.

Phase V: Five ways to find meaning in your transition and move on

1. Talk to people whom you trust
   - How should I express pride in my courage of the heart?
2. Commit to regular activities providing relief
   - What do I add to my work or personal-life activities that will demonstrate what I want and hope for?
3. Create your own transition story
   - How do I explain how my transition ended and how it led to a new beginning?
4. Find guides to help you navigate your transition
   - How do new guides help me move through and beyond my transition?
5. Learn about what you need to heal your heart
   - How do I demonstrate that I have moved on from my transition?
   - What actions are key reminders of the courage of my heart?

On the next page is a summary chart for Part One.

In the appendix, page 129 you can find Courage of the Heart worksheets and related questions for each of the five phases. The worksheets are offered as a reminder of the kinds of questions that will help you to build your unplanned-transition skill set and your courage of the heart.

SUMMARY CHART

Dealing with unplanned life-altering transitions

How do I build courage of the heart?	I. Accepting the emotional impact of an unexpected work or life event	II. Getting the support you need to rebuild your confidence	III. Building new routines as you explore new options	IV. Giving back to people who have helped you	V. Finding meaning in your transition and moving on
1. Talk to people whom you trust	What are the unknowns? What do I no longer have? What do I miss?	Who is there for me now, and who is not?	Who can I count on to give me feedback on my progress? How do I ask for feedback?	How do I reciprocate to the people who have helped me?	How should I express pride in my courage of the heart?
2. Commit to regular activities providing relief	What are the knowns? What do I still have? What do I cherish and will do more of?	Which activities give me a boost now?	How do I build these activities into my life? What can I be sure of continuing to do?	How do I give back to myself and to others? How can I be better prepared for the next transition?	What do I add to my work or personal-life activities to demonstrate what I want and hope for?
3. Create your own transition story	When/what was my defining moment? What were the signs/signals that this was going to happen?	How do I explain what I am doing now? What should I call it? What is this chapter in my life?	How do I explain the benefits of these new routines?	How have I benefited from this transition? What have I compromised through this transition?	How do I explain how my transition ended and how it led to a new beginning?
4. Find guides to help you navigate your transition	How do I find out how I am doing? How do I check my physical, mental and emotional health?	How do I rebuild my faith in myself? How do I spend my free time?	Which routines will support my moving beyond this transition?	Who will help me sustain my healed heart?	How do new guides help me move through and beyond my transition?
5. Learn about what you need to heal your heart	Whom can I talk to with experience of this kind of life-altering transition? How have others moved beyond their transitions?	What are the main barriers I am facing while moving through this transition?	How will I know when I am ready to move beyond the transition?	What lessons did I learn that help guide what I do next?	How do I demonstrate that I have moved on from my transition? What actions are key reminders of the courage of my heart?

PART TWO
COURAGE OF THE MIND

PART TWO

COURAGE OF THE MIND

Choosing to plan life-enhancing transitions

Those of us in the baby-boom generation are approaching an age when we begin to contemplate what we have done with our lives and start asking ourselves, "What next?" We realize our careers may not last forever, and wonder how we will adjust to working less or not working at all after identifying ourselves with our work for so long. This is also a time when our personal lives may become more complex, whether in terms of having to care for aging parents or dealing with age-related health issues of our own.

Having been born at the start of the baby boom myself, I have always felt that, as a group, we have been ground-breakers for many social experiments, both at work and in our personal lives. We have orchestrated and participated in re-engineered workplaces, and many of us have ventured into uncharted waters in terms of our personal lives. Now we are about to become the largest generation of senior citizens in history. How will we put our stamp on this period of life?

How to look at transitions in terms of building courage of the mind

Planned transitions begin when you decide you want to consider new or different ways of working or living. You may want to change jobs, or move to a new city, or simply change the way you spend your day, ideally making your routines more in sync with new or special activities in your life.

In the Western world, we are reared in a purposeful way, and many use the same mindset to plan their work lives. Purposeful or planned approaches usually have a sequence of proven or tested steps that follow a logical and rationally devised strategy. All of this takes skills that will help you develop a plan and implement it—in other words, courage of the mind. You will progress if you are determined, disciplined and able to ask for help from people who may inspire you or offer their moral support. The mind's courage gives you purpose, and directs you through to the end of the transition feeling rejuvenated.

A life of planned transitions can also include turns of events that could not have been predicted. The main justification for being organized about a career path is based on the rewards it could bring: new opportunities, and greater responsibilities and pay. Most believe there are logical steps they can take when they plan their careers or even their lives. And yet, we all acknowledge there are many surprises or unexpected circumstances that have great influence. For example, a common expression for successful job-finders is, "I was at the right place at the right time" or, "When an opportunity landed in my lap, I seized it."

In our personal lives, we can often allow a more spontaneous flow of change and adjustment, particularly as we age. It is also ideal to have a more spontaneous approach to planned work transitions. Spontaneity will inject more humour and

playfulness into the process, and make it feel more like your own personal adventure.

My time in India: experiencing the benefits of being open to chance

When I emphasize the importance of serendipity or being open to chance in transitions, it reminds me of the life perspective I accepted wholeheartedly while living in India for two years. Living there taught me to allow for an emerging experience of life. This was a big shift from the perspective I had had most of my life, which was highly planned and organized into logical sequences.

In India, the events of a day were never certain. There were many simple interruptions, such as brief power shutdowns or difficult weather conditions. Whenever you ventured onto the road, you were sure to be met with unexpected traffic barriers, and, on one trip, we lost our direct route when a flooding river suddenly submerged a bridge. A multitude of unexpected circumstances influenced how we lived, and I learned to accept the constant change, adjusting or making compromises to whatever had been planned.

I also got to know some remarkable people whose lives were very fluid. I found that living with and welcoming the benefits of serendipity came naturally to me. However, when I came back to Canada, I was out of sync with the routines I had left behind. The culture shock was disorienting, and not one I expected. However, I think I understand it now in terms of all that I am learning about transitions. Namely, even if transitions are planned, like our stay in India, events and emotions emerge or evolve in ways that could not have been predicted at the outset.

Planning and re-planning a transition

Transitions at work and in life are often planned and then

re-planned. Whatever the stimulus in the first instance, often the circumstances that lead to a change cannot be fully laid out in advance. Every experience of a planned transition will include planned and unplanned elements.

The period of planning for a work or life transition allows you to make choices among activities or routines that are important for you to continue. Ideally, you will want to take as much time as you need so the experience allows you to feel you are benefiting from what you are learning and discovering along the way. The experience of your life-enhancing transition will also build skills or experiences you will be able to call on for any future transitions.

Many people I interviewed described their planned transitions as times that were re-energizing and encouraging. Along with a sense of hope, some also described days when the prospect of change made their doubts overshadow their hopes. Many were uncertain about the best timing or what their experience after the transition would be like. However, their sensing of possibilities propelled them to keep the process moving along and not lose their enthusiasm.

At the end of each chapter in Part Two are a list of questions to use as a guide for each phase. These are offered as prompts to enhance your experience of your transition and activities as you plan them.

Phase I: Deciding to make a work or life change

Early on in my research for this book, I began to understand why planned and unplanned transitions are so different. The stories I heard revealed patterns prompted more by how the transition began than any other factor. When the start was planned, it was a hopeful scenario. When the start was unplanned, it was often, as one individual put it, a "catastrophe."

At the beginning of every interview, I asked people how

their transition had started and whether they had planned it or it had come as a surprise. What was interesting to discover was that many of the planned transitions were a hybrid, with planned and unplanned elements.

Starting out

In his 1991 book on organizational transitions, *Managing Transitions: Making the Most of Change* (re-released in an expanded version in 2003), the famous North American transition guru, William Bridges, coined a description of work-related transitions in terms of three distinct phases: "Ending, Losing and Letting Go," "The Neutral Zone" and "The New Beginning."

My friend Bill, a ghostwriter, looks at planned transitions in a metaphorical way. He believes the experience of undertaking a new creative venture (such as writing a book) is like setting out into the woods to search for what you want, armed with a bow and arrow. You are looking for your target, but meanwhile, you are unable to see very far in any direction, and the tall trees and dark pockets of silence are a bit intimidating. Ideally, you would like to fire an arrow and hit the bull's-eye immediately, but, as Bill explained, such a journey is best begun by aiming your arrows at many targets. Wherever an arrow makes a solid hit is where you draw a bull's-eye. In other words, you really cannot know where you are headed until you make several attempts and then choose the goal that feels right to you.

Questions to ask yourself before planning a transition

The appendix includes a chart called Questions To Ask Yourself Before Planning a Transition. Answering the questions will help you to find out how you feel about the prospect of a transition. The questions will also help you to understand what impact your potential transition may have on your family and friends.

My research showed that planned transitions, as compared to unplanned ones, are not as stressful. In addition, planned transitions usually required preparation and happened more quickly. The more difficult transitions also brought significant personal lessons. Most people who made these kinds of difficult transitions also changed the way they lived their lives after their transitions.

Three reasons for deciding to plan a change

The transition stories I heard fell into three main groupings. When people had the opportunity to make a change, they had different reasons for wanting it. These reasons influenced their transition. Here are the three main types of changes:

- work focus: doing the same job elsewhere;
- personal-talent focus: finding a dream job; and
- life and work combination focus: reinventing both work and personal-life circumstances.

If any of these three reasons are relevant to you, here are some things to consider before you begin to devise your plan. The chart on the next page lists the three reasons for planning a change, along with tips in each of three categories: how to prepare for the start of your transition; researching options; and anticipating what the post-transition will be like.

Three goals		Suggestions for the process of your planned transition		
		HOW TO PREPARE FOR THE START OF YOUR TRANSITION	RESEARCHING OPTIONS	ANTICIPATING WHAT THE POST-TRANSITION WILL BE LIKE
WORK FOCUS: I want to do the same job elsewhere		Refer to popular career-change self-help books and workbooks that provide a step-by-step guide. Have you a plan to make the change? Are you open to chance or surprises that might present new possibilities?	Narrow your options: • Industry (private sector or public; government or not-for-profit) • Location • Role/position • Salary range • Benefits • Size of organization	What are you planning to give up and what will you add or reinvigorate? You might want to make a list of the kinds of activities you can look forward to or create.
PERSONAL-TALENT FOCUS: I want to find my dream job		Experiment with metaphors or descriptions of the dream job, your role, and routines. What would be an ideal workday?	Talk to people who claim to have their dream job. What makes each so unique? How would you build your own dream job if one does not exist?	List your expectations and think about how you will know when you have found your dream job.
LIFE AND WORK COMBINATION FOCUS: I want to reinvent my work and personal life		Look at the daily mix of time spent at work and pursuing personal interests. How do you move from one to the other to allow yourself enough time for both?	Will the reinvention affect work life and personal life equally? If not, begin by considering options where the change will be felt immediately.	Describe a day in your life when the reinvention has begun. What kinds of weekly routines can you look forward to?

The focus for change

Doing the same job somewhere else

When people decide to take their skills and experience to another work setting, there are many reasons for planning such changes. Some want a break from working in a very large organization.

After being a partner in a large law firm for 25 years, David wanted to work in a smaller office and have more free time. Because his partners were resistant to the idea, he began by trying to arrange his workload so he had more flexibility. In the end, however, this proved too difficult to maintain, and David gave his notice. He described his confidence during this transition as a key to making the shift possible. As he put it, "I may not be right, but I am not in doubt." David spent a few years in a temporary space until he had a clear idea of how he could continue to practice law on his own terms.

Other people reach a career roadblock and realize a planned transition might bring them unexpected benefits, even if the prospect of change is intimidating. The people I talked to often found their lives had more balance after such a transition.

Philip admits he was upset when he was overlooked for a promotion. Almost immediately, he began to plot his exit from the advertising agency where he worked, even though he did so with great regret. He found a senior position in a smaller agency, and although he found he was occasionally haunted by the fear of failure during the early months of his new job, he quickly became energized and enthusiastic about his new responsibilities. His changed work circumstances also brought about changes in the rest of his life. He had more time for personal pursuits and to be with his children, and as a result, he gained new perspective: he could, he said, "do just as well with one-quarter of the angst." Philip's concluding thought on his transition would be the advice he now gives to others who come for tips on their own potential work changes: "It's never as catastrophic as you think it is. Life goes on, and you don't fall off the edge of a cliff."

Often, people making a planned transition encounter setbacks they were not expecting. Many transitions, for example, take far more time than anyone bargains for. Initially, this may feel frightening, but the upside is that the weeks or even months spent looking for a new job also allow the person to consult mentors and learn from the experience of people who have made a similar shift. And once again, the transitions frequently had other, personal benefits.

Raymond had worked for a large construction company for many years. When he was essentially demoted, he felt rejected, and finally decided to find another job. Not knowing how long it would take to find something new proved difficult for him. Raymond expressed it this way: "I discovered how important working is to me." When he talked to people who had gone through similar transitions, he found that "the time frame was a challenge they all had experienced." In the end, it took him about a year and a half to find a position with a smaller company that had the flexible and resourceful work atmosphere he wanted. Once he began working there, he realized he never wanted to be part of a large, rigid and politically charged enterprise again.

Other work-related transitions can simply be more difficult than anticipated. When the work transition impacts our life and family, often the experience has unexpected consequences. Everyone participating in a physical relocation, for example, will be affected.

As an architect, Charles had already gone through several work transitions in his life, all of which had gone relatively smoothly. He could not have predicted that his last one would prove to be quite the opposite. His new job involved moving his family—his wife, Heather, and their two young children— to Amsterdam. Because the cost of living was higher than he and Heather had expected, she took on a teaching job, something she hadn't done since their children were born. This meant there were profound changes both in their work and personal lives. Their relocation was made additionally stressful by the unexpected death of Heather's

father soon after they moved.

Charles's experience left him with a new appreciation of how his current work change had not followed the pattern of any of his earlier transitions. He explained his understanding this way: "At a certain point, life presents a bill." In other words, he felt this transition was the point where he paid his dues. This time the transition had more downsides than upsides.

Like Charles, others talked about how they ultimately found reasons to justify the upheaval. They described how, as time passed, they gained a new perspective on the full experience of planning and making change. As they reflected on the lessons learned, they realized their next transition might be planned differently to avoid what went wrong. A few typical remarks: *"It's very important to set priorities and be in constant touch with how you are doing in the process—take risks like vitamins"; "I would have better organized my personal life situation if I had realized what it would take to make the adjustment"; "Having the nerve to do this came from an altruistic place that gave it the extra push. If a transition is for the right reasons, it is powerful to be daring—there is magic in power."*

Sometimes, unplanned events force people to acknowledge that a transition is necessary. Frequently, though, the people I talked to felt that, despite being initially pushed into taking action, they had taken charge of the change and it had been a positive one.

Cheryl had been feeling exhausted and weak for months before she was diagnosed with chronic fatigue syndrome. She had not been happy at work for some time—she was a buyer for a major department store—but her boss tormented her and her colleagues relentlessly. It wasn't until she took a short holiday that she realized she had to quit. Cheryl had difficulty finding a permanent job with the seniority and salary she was accustomed to, she was still unwell, and as a result, she went into debt. After three tough years, her health improved significantly and so did her professional life. She was able to take on a few special projects

for smaller stores, and because of their success, decided to remain self-employed. Her business is now flourishing, and she is happy to have a new, more satisfying work life. She has also learned, as she says, "Change is something to be embraced."

Working in a high-powered job, as many people discover, can be both a blessing and a curse. But here again, a change in work circumstances can end up bringing unexpected personal benefits.

Sarah had an executive sales position in a large printing firm, with all the perks that came with it: a sizeable salary, a car allowance and bonuses when the company did well. But at a certain point, she realized she was burned out. She knew leaving her corporate life would be a big financial and personal adjustment—"They seduced me into a certain lifestyle"—but she decided to leave and look for something else. She began her search, but she had not expected the job market would be so tight. After a few frustrating months, she decided to take a sabbatical and volunteer in her local community hospital and only take on short work contracts. Sarah came to realize she had compromised her personal interests and time for friends and family in her last job. In fact, some neighbours and friends told her they had not seen her human side for a long while. After a yearlong transition, Sarah finally found a new job that allowed her to preserve her new personal priorities. She vowed she would never compromise these again. "I wish," she said, "I had been more honest with myself earlier."

Finding a dream job

Anyone whose transition allowed them to try a new kind of work about which they were passionate talked about their transition as allowing them to fulfill a dream. These were often people who had saved in order to provide a financial cushion that would allow them to experiment for at least six months. Whenever people had the privilege of testing a

dream, they described the upsides of this experience first. They are energizing stories.

Mark had always wanted to try his hand at being an entrepreneur. He finally reached a point in his career when, after 10 years working at an office-supplies company, he resigned to take the chance on his dream. He talked about it this way: "You say to yourself, 'Who am I? What am I good at? And what's going to map against my interests?'" He was excited about his prospects, and explained that, for him, the stress was positive, what he called, "the buzz of the journey." He admitted that at times it was lonely but, overall, he welcomed the pressure of the unknown, of being outside his comfort zone. He called his transition story "Expanding Horizons."

Some people make extremely radical changes in their lives that end up bringing them great satisfaction. One way of trying to reinvent your work life is to go back to school. Whatever your passion—arts and culture, business, photography—retraining is often a catalyst for a new kind of work. The most dramatic part of such retraining transitions is that every element of your daily routine is changed. Some people even travelled out of town over extended periods of time.

Franca decided to get a graduate degree in architecture in a city that was far from where she lived with her husband, Yves. The cost meant she and Yves had to sell their home and downsize to a one-bedroom apartment. Fortunately, Yves supported Franca in her getting on with her dream, and went along with the house sale and Franca's weekly commuting. However, their marriage began to falter when he challenged her on the amount of schoolwork she did when she returned home on weekends. Franca realized she had to move between two worlds, and could not bring her study world home. This saved their relationship. When she looked back on what she had been through to remake her career, she realized it had altered both her work and personal life. After successfully completing her degree, she found that what now mattered to her

was no longer career advancement but career stability, and a group of coworkers who brought out the best in her. That was the highlight of achieving her dream: the people she came across and studied with. "The peer group that brings out the best in you is remarkable."

Miranda had been contemplating moving out of the corporate fast track as an investment banker for some time because her health was being severely compromised by the pace and demands of her job. She had been taking yoga and meditation classes for a number of years, and her transition began with the decision to leave her job and build a new work life around her interest in yoga. After she resigned, she opened her own studio. Being self-employed, she limited the number of clients she accepted, and the new business offered both the freedom and flexibility she wanted. As she said, "I took the chance to explore the depths of my own spirituality as a complement to my work." She advises others to "really listen to your spirit—often it is cloaked with cobwebs linked to the ego."

Like other transitions, finding your dream job frequently gives rise to other changes in your life. What some might call a dream job is a way of creating a job change that brings all the parts of your life together. However, getting a dream job—like any other job—can also bring surprises.

Isabella was excited when she was offered a job running a small joint-venture food business, bringing together people from remote cultural and historical backgrounds. She saw in this a unique opportunity to combine her interest in other cultures with her organizational abilities. Unfortunately, after familiarizing herself with the operation, she discovered the place was in chaos. She had a tough choice to make: tell the board of the enterprise to close it down before more losses occurred, or start to rebuild. Isabella knew if she began to remake the enterprise, she would have to work at least 10 hours a day for six months. She did just that. The first step was to find a small flat near the business so she could be close by if problems arose. She and her family lived in a community some distance from the operation, so she started

commuting home on weekends. Her hard work paid off—the business started showing signs of profit. It made it past the first cycle of debt refinancing and is still a going concern.

When Sheila quit her job with an import-export company to work on her own, the network of international contacts she had built meant she was in demand almost immediately. However, she quickly realized these new work opportunities took her away from home for weeks at a time. This prompted her to make changes in the rest of her life. She had been renting out two apartments in her house, but this was no longer practical or worthwhile. She sold her house and bought another, smaller one where she had no financial obligations. Her advice to anyone about transitions is, "If you don't manage your life, it will manage you."

Sometimes, the dream that people imagine is not sustainable. However, the transition can still be of benefit as a bridge to self-knowledge and perhaps another dream that will work.

Nona and her husband, Lorne, moved to the U.S, to live in the city where his telecom corporation was headquartered. Nona gave up her role running a horse stable north of Ottawa. She and Lorne had been partners in the stables, and his work move coincided with their decision to sell. Nona was ready to move on, although regretted having to give up riding. They both hoped their new life and work would put them on a path to getting back to a rural setting later on, having saved some extra money as well. Unfortunately, Lorne's company participated in a merger within six months of their setting up a new home, and Lorne's job was cut. A good severance package did cushion the blow, but they were uncertain they could manage to stay in their new community. Nona found a well-paying job in a large corporation, and gradually, Lorne found more and more consulting contracts. But within a few years, Nona lost her job when her department was eliminated. She decided to retrain in a totally different field—holistic nutrition—and also resumed her horse riding. She realizes now that riding is an activity she will never leave again.

She does not know where her retraining will take her, but for now, she has dropped the idea of ever going back into the corporate world.

One interesting aspect of making a transition to a job you've always dreamed about is they are not always easy to plan. Often it is serendipity—along with the person's determination and courage—that allows the transition to move forward.

Harold calls his transition "planned impulsive." He became interested in web development and database management in 1995 after completing an MA in economics. His dream was to build a small data- and Internet-management consulting business, but he had to wait several months to fulfill his dream because he needed to save up to buy the necessary computers. However, his timing was perfect because it coincided with the start of the Internet boom. The business is now a thriving enterprise, and Harold has time to enjoy his passion for playing ice hockey.

Similarly, the next story illustrates the need for careful thought and preparation as well as the importance of being open to chance encounters.

Janice had worked for the post office her entire working life. Although she was at the peak of her career and salary, she was also sure that, eventually, she'd see her job eliminated or drastically changed. Her union seniority was her only job protection. As a single parent supporting two university-aged children, the prospect of being out of work haunted her. She sold her home and opted to rent, getting rid of the weight of a mortgage and other debts, and the relief from these financial pressures gave her time to rethink her work life.

Janice moved through her transition with the help of a few trusted friends and a career coach. After a few months, she realized that, "Suddenly, new career ideas seemed to come from every direction," including a question from the real-estate agent who had sold her home: "Have you ever considered getting your

real-estate license?" The idea appealed to her immediately.

Janet did not tell her employer about her plans. She pursued her real-estate studies, and when it came time to take the exams, she asked for, and received, a special unpaid leave, which she pooled with her vacation time. She passed the exam on the first try. Colleagues and friends introduced her to several real-estate companies, and she joined a well-established firm, a decision she described as a "leap of faith." Right away, it was clear that the real-estate business was her dream job.

Janice was sorry she hadn't initiated this transition years earlier, although, she adds, "Serendipity played so much of a part in it." She also feels she is a better parent, financially and emotionally, to her children. Her new work has also, she says, "exponentially expanded [her] financial possibilities," giving her "renewed hope and contentment."

Reinventing work and personal circumstances

These transitions are very different from any other type of transition. They lead to working and living in circumstances that look and feel very different from what people have left behind. The changes are more than incremental ones. Deciding to make your work and life better and more personally meaningful can happen at any time in a career. If you think about the acceptance of a more holistic approach many people are taking to their mental and physical health, a career transition can be approached in the same way.

Melinda took a long time to decide to move to a competitor in the garment-manufacturing industry in which she worked. One of the reasons she hesitated was that the new company was not located in her home city. Many of her and her family's routines would be disrupted. Initially, Melinda and her husband, who had been retired for some time, were put off by the possibility of her commuting three days a week, since it would involve even more travel than her current international travel requirements.

However, the prospect of a significant promotion and increase in salary convinced her to accept.

Before she agreed to her new role, Melinda drew up some conditions: she could work at home on Mondays and Fridays, and only have to work out of town from Tuesdays through Thursdays. The company also committed to no weekend e-mail, since she was going to be working much longer days when she out of town.

She has found the new work routines have enhanced her whole family's life. Working from home allows her to have spontaneous lunches with friends in the neighbourhood. And no weekend work, which had been a burden to her in her previous job, means Saturday and Sunday can be devoted to herself, her family and friends.

Reflecting on her transition, Melinda admitted that when she had asked for input from people who knew her well, they wondered why she had waited so long. "I now have a sense of freedom," she said.

Some work/life transitions, like other types of transitions, begin unexpectedly, and then unexpected events also occur during the transition. These will not only compromise the work transition but also prompt larger questions about life.

Phyllis was an up-and-coming dancer. Her transition began when the ballet she was in reached the end of its run. Unfortunately, this coincided with her separation from her partner, with whom she'd been having emotional difficulties for some time. The start of her transition was very stressful and emotionally draining. She said she felt "shipwrecked," because her lack of another dancing job and the failure of her relationship combined to make her lose all confidence in herself. With her parents' support, Phyllis went back to studying acting (she had been a prize-winning actress until her dance career took off), which led her to build a new work plan of giving acting lessons herself. Thanks to this renewed self-confidence, she was also able to reconcile with her partner on new terms. She looked back on her transition as the catalyst that brought important and

sustainable changes to her work and personal life. Her retelling of her transition story included a recommendation to others who are attempting to reinvent themselves: "Treat yourself gently and with compassion."

Something as seemingly inconsequential as a change in the atmosphere at work can be a catalyst that brings about a major work/life transition. Planning a work change does not usually have great urgency if everything else in life is in balance. However, sometimes unusual and unpredicted work circumstances do create a sense of urgency to make change happen.

Within five years of joining an accounting firm, Ted was promoted to partner. His work life became much more demanding, which took its toll on his family, but Ted felt not only loyalty and commitment to the firm but also a great deal of pride in the work he did.

However, the partnership unexpectedly started to unravel, due to personality clashes among the founding partners. Ted tried not to let it interfere with his work, since the financial consequences made the prospect of leaving the company an unappealing option. Ultimately, after months of experimenting with ways to relieve the stress of his workload and the work discord, he finally decided that the financial incentive to stay was not worth compromising his own health and the well-being of his family.

Ted developed a financial plan to get him and his family through the transition and then left the firm. From several new job offers, he chose a position at the university where he had graduated. This meant moving his family and starting over, but as a result, he and his wife have a lifestyle and living rhythm that make their life better for themselves and their young daughter. Ted says, "My work is now more aligned with my personal life and values."

These transitions do cause disruption. But for the people who know what they want, they usually allow themselves the time to try to get it right. The support of your partner is key, since any change you make in your work and life will

inevitably affect them, too.

Robert's decision to start a travel agency in his home city, after years of travelling all over North America as the representative of a major airline, dramatically affected his personal life. His wife, Holly, and their baby were suddenly much more a part of his world. Unexpectedly, even though Robert decided he would like to share more in the parenting of their child, he and his wife began to face challenges in their marriage. His wife encouraged him to resolve their differences by seeing a marital counsellor. Meanwhile, Robert's business had been slow in taking off. After a year, the long-term prospects began to improve, but Robert described the benefits of his transition primarily in terms of how things improved at home. His partnership with Holly began to work much better, and he credits her with giving him the kind of support and encouragement that made the transition possible. In his own words, "You can't do it without a partner – involve your partner, be open and listen."

While your partner's support during a transition is important, sometimes it can be a long time coming.

Ever since she was a young woman, Violet had dreamed of finding work that would help the less-fortunate in society. Instead, worried about financial instability, she got an MBA and found a job with a national hotel chain, where she quickly worked her way up to senior management. When she finally considered taking time off to plan a much-needed change, she discovered how much of a stigma there was to taking a break from a job. Despite her spotless work record, the company simply wouldn't hear of her leaving her job for any extended period of time.

Violet also discovered that her husband, Ron, was not as supportive as she had expected. When she found a new position as senior administrator of a national charity, and Ron came to see what essential work this organization was accomplishing, he finally saw the benefits of the change and understood Violet much better when she said, "It is so important to follow what you have convictions about. Getting emotionally stirred up about your

work — there's nothing better."

One of the frequent benefits of a transition is that people realize, during and after the experience, that they themselves are stronger and more resilient than they had thought.

Louis counted on his wife's financial support to get him launched in a consulting business after a long career in local government. He talked about the fear of the unknown in the beginning, a state he called his "solitary walk that created liberty and loneliness." He found this kind of isolation difficult, but overall, the thrill for Louis came from his realization that he was much stronger than he had given himself credit for. "When a couple of things start to work," he said, "it's such a high."

Sometimes, people postpone a transition for many years, but eventually, they are able to make the move they have long wanted.

Jasper did not have a defining moment that helped him decide to make a change. Rather, he said, it was a gradual realization that he had compromised the life he had led in his 20s and 30s as a musician and he wanted to go back to it. It was not something he could make happen in a short time. He had worked as a high-school teacher for over 15 years, and wanted to make sure he could leave with a decent pension. When we talked, the work transition had been underway for eight years and was almost over. Jasper's personal life was also in a new phase, with a new partner and new home where he had set up a studio for practicing. He told me, "I am taking my life back."

Phase I: Five ways to decide to make a work or life change

1. Career/life patterns: work/play
   - Have you experienced work or life transitions before? If yes, what do you remember?
2. Relationships
   - Who among your friends and family will support you through the transition?

3. Vision/goals: What will the results look like?
   - What are your dreams for the future, beyond your transition?
4. Self-awareness: Who am I?
   - How well do you think you know yourself?
   - How would people who know you well describe you?
5. The kind of transition experience
   - Have you ever planned or prepared for a work or life change?

Phase II: Defining your transition experience

"The least livable life is the one without coherence—nothing connects, nothing means anything. Stories make connections. They allow us to see our past, our present and our future as interrelated and purposeful. We seek out stories which enhance this process."

This quote captures the main theme of Daniel Taylor's 1996 book, *The Healing Power of Stories: Creating Yourself Through the Stories of Your Life*. It is useful to consider the start of your transition as the beginning of a new chapter in your life. With the changes you are about to make, you may find it easier to describe what is happening in the form of a story. Looking back over how you got to where you are today sets the stage for the next chapter of your work or life.

Collect your thoughts and build your story with trusted confidants or a professional coach. In this way, you can find the words and ideas you feel comfortable with and rehearse them before anyone asks you to tell your story in a more public way, because you may find you feel self-conscious about telling your story if you are not expecting to. For instance, some people told me that at holiday gatherings they felt they had to tell all before they were ready to do so, when family members, out of interest and genuine concern, asked them questions.

Taking a backward glance: reviewing your career or life history

The first step in your transition planning process is to

review your life and work story. As you start planning your transition, it's important to understand the sequence of steps that brought you to this point in your life and work. This involves some serious soul-searching. You will likely recall very positive memories and some less joyful, even painful ones. Try to look honestly and objectively at all of your experiences. Your goal is to understand the choices you've made in your work and life, and to understand the result.

I work as a career coach with people to help them review their career history. In this chapter, I will be your career coach. You'll have the opportunity to work through a series of questions to help you understand your career. Telling your career story to another person who can be an objective listener can help you to understand it better. At some point, you may decide you want to work through the questions with someone (e.g. a trusted friend, colleague, mentor or career counsellor) who can act as a sounding board, be a guide to help you set realistic goals and give you feedback on the options you are considering.

The questions that follow are aimed at understanding the sequence of events in a 20-year career, from adolescence to the present. If your career is shorter, then just work as far as you can. Your answers to these questions will help you create your life story at work (what you do for income or financial rewards) and play (what you do for personal fulfillment—in other words, social, political, cultural, athletic, artistic or spiritual activities).

Get a scrapbook and use each page to cover a five-year period in your work and life. Record your answers to the questions for each time period, and then gather up concrete records of those five-year periods with anything you can find: personal photos, mementos, birthday cards, letters of employment, endorsements, special records of accomplishment. Try to give each five-year period a name and put that title at the top of each page. These become the unique chapters in your story. Of course, looking back on your life, you may have had a single year that deserves a chapter all of its own!

Taking a backward glance: reviewing your career or life history

There are two kinds of questions – those related to your personal spontaneous "play" with a "P" after the number, and those related to your work life with a "W" after the number.

1-**P** What did you do as an adolescent in your spare time when you were not at school?

_____

_____

2-**W** When did you get your first paid job (part-time or full-time)? How old were you? What work did you do? Who hired you? What skills did you gain from this experience?

_____

_____

3-**P** When you were in high school, what extra-curricular activities did you enjoy? What made you choose these? Did you continue these beyond high school?

_____

_____

4-**W** When you chose a course of study at college or university, did you have a career in mind? How did you decide on your first job after graduating from college or university?

_____

_____

5-**P** While you were in your 20s, what did you and your closest friends do together to enjoy yourselves outside of work?

_____

_____

Looking back on the first 10 years of your career

6-**W** Thinking of your first 10 years of full-time work, describe one or more things you did that made you very proud.

_____

_____

6a)-**W**   If you had more than one role or position during your first 10 years of full-time work, what were the reasons for your changes? How did you experience the transitions between each new role?

_____

_____

7-**P**   During these first 10 years of work what did you do out-side work to enjoy yourself?

_____

_____

7a)- **P**   Did any events or activities in your life outside of work influence your working life during these first 10 years of work? If so, did any of them influence decisions you made about changes at work?

_____

_____

Your work and personal life beyond the first 10 years of your career

8-**W** Thinking about your next five or more years of work, describe one or more things you did that made you very proud.

_____

_____

9-**P**   During this same period, what did you do outside of work to enjoy yourself?

_____

_____

10-**W**   If you ever planned a change in your work life, did you benefit from some support as you moved through the transition? If so, what kind of support did you have? As you think about the transition you want to make now, could you count on these same supports again?

_____

_____

With your rekindled memories of important phases in your work or life to date, think about any previous transitions that were important. Your experience of earlier transitions will help you plan your next one.

The support of others during a transition

Once you have decided to make your work or life transition, the next step is to decide what kinds of supports might help you with the experience. The people I interviewed turned to many types of supports as they faced new and different challenges. Because change is stressful, you may benefit from taking extra time for activities that will offset your stress. Going to a movie, hiking, singing in a choir, taking the dog for a walk or doing a fitness routine are all ideal.

Most people I interviewed said the biggest source of help and support for them during their transitions was people they trusted. They said they needed to find people they could count on.

Some were not prepared for surprises, such as friends or family being discouraging about their making a change. When you start to tell people about your plans, some may

be indifferent or pessimistic because they are jealous of your options or are being overprotective of you. Some people may discover that a friendship has been based on the prestige attached to whom you work for and not on who you are. Sometimes people who start a transition are disappointed when friends they thought they could depend on do not encourage or support them. These disappointments are hurtful, but it is actually better to find out who these people are early in your transition so you do not count on them in the future.

In the appendix, you can find a chart called People Supports to identify the kinds of supports you may need for your transition and where you might find them.

Starting your transition experience

Starting a work or life transition usually adds some unexpected new stresses. Most of the people I interviewed experienced some stress, even when they planned their transition and were very positive about its eventual outcome. Try to time the start of your transition to coincide with a time when you expect minimal stresses in your routines. For example, some people scheduled the start of their transitions to coincide with a time of year when they could enjoy favourite outdoor activities. These activities became part of their transitions, helping them to relieve their stress and recharge their energy and enthusiasm.

Others planned a transition for a time of year when holiday gatherings or family commitments would not distract them. It is probably not wise to start a transition when you are exhausted or anxious because of personal or work situations. As well, some people felt they simply did not want to deal with a lot of questions about their decision in the first few weeks. Try to lessen your personal commitments. Free up extra time to get yourself ready.

Deciding how to begin your transition

Charting your course for change may allow you to identify how you would like it to end. Ideally, you want to make the experience a meaningful and memorable one. Some people were keen to start their transition with a break from all past routines. For example, some moved and others went on trips. Some who were regular fitness fanatics added more time to their daily or weekly exercise regimen.

In the appendix, you can find worksheets and related questions for each of the four phases. These worksheets are offered as a reminder of the kind of questions that will help you to build your planned-transition skill set and your courage of the mind.

Measuring your progress

There are several ways to measure your progress:
- Set a timetable and try to keep to it.
- List the things you want to do within a period of time (days or weeks) and try to carry them out in a flexible order (let chance play a part in the sequence).
- Check in periodically with trusted people (colleague, mentor, coach, counsellor) to review your progress.

Keep in mind that, although you are drawing up a timetable, you should also be flexible. You may need to change the order of your transition activities as you move through the first few months and gather more information. You may also benefit from a situation that brings new opportunities serendipitously.

Defining moments

The start of a planned transition is a significant personal crossroads. The people I talked to often spoke about a "defining moment" of their transition. They gave a detailed description of their personal epiphany ("I was sitting at

dinner party and I just knew I had to take that training program" or, "I realized I wasn't prepared to put up with my boss any longer"). They remembered what the crossroads felt like, and as the details began to emerge, they said it was like focusing a camera.

As your transition begins, you may feel like you are off to a fresh start. Many transitionees described this as "opening new doors" or "expanding horizons." If you start your transition with this mindset, your enthusiasm and energy will help sustain you through any unexpected barriers or obstacles.

You will likely feel anxious about the unknowns. Feeling worried or anxious is perfectly normal and understandable. Unconsciously, you may not want to start your transition, and may even put it off. Postponing a transition more than once may be a signal you are not ready. Your start does not have to be dramatic, but it should be clean, by which I mean, don't have too many loose ends before you go forward. It's probably good to pay off your credit cards. You might need the extra cushion of credit when buying a new wardrobe for job interviews. You may also feel eager to take the first opportunity that comes along, simply for financial reasons. Best to know you have the time and financial cushion to take extra time if you want it. You will regret making a decision too early in the process, especially if it does not completely feel right.

There are often intangibles that you can only judge instinctively. Let your instincts guide you through a change. Often they are the most authentic and genuine clues you can rely on. At the same time, don't feel everything has to be perfect before you can begin creating a new story.

The transition may have less routine than other periods of your life. However, the experience will give you practice at skills that will likely come in handy again.

Alex's transition included changes in both his personal and work lives. He was building a new business as well as grieving the death

of his sister from cancer. His own advice to other transitionees was this: "When you face it, just take each day and deal with it as it is. Don't ignore it and don't feel sorry for yourself."

Here are some questions to consider when you are coming up with how you will tell your transition story.

Phase II: Five ways to define your transition experience

1. Career/life patterns: work/play
   - Which activities from either your work or play do you want to preserve or eliminate during your transition?
2. Relationships
   - Whom will you ask to support you or be a catalyst for you as you begin your transition?
3. Vision/goals: What will the future look like?
   - How would you define your goals for your transition? What results are you hoping for?
4. Self-awareness: Who am I?
   - Are you an idealist or a pragmatist about what you can change?
5. The kind of transition experience
   - How will you keep track of your progress during your transition? Will you set a timetable?

Phase III: Telling people about your transition plan

Before getting your transition underway, you probably thought about earlier transitions and what you did to get them started. If there are ways to make the transition part of a new chapter in your life, it will help if you can explain what you have planned before you begin. A key message in your news about making a change and starting a transition is revealing your true feelings and hopes.

When you have made the decision to change your work or life situation, you may feel a combination of eager anticipation and fear of an unknown future. Your personal

emotional barometer will help you decide how to explain the experience.

Creating a name for your transition

Once you have begun to imagine a new work or life situation, you may want to give your transition a name. The name is your way of presenting the official start of the transition and confirming your commitment to yourself. Even if the actual beginning of your transition is days or weeks later, this naming will announce its start to others. People who have encouraged your decision to make a change may have been sounding boards for you. Best to tell these people first what you are calling your transition.

I encouraged the people I interviewed to name their transition so we could refer to it in the context of our talk. This request often seemed to stump them. They were not sure what the name should convey. However, after they named their transition, they realized it helped to capture their experience in a few words, like the title of a chapter in their life.

Some people gave their transition a name that put a negative spin on the experience: "It was like the pain of childbirth" or "Leaving my intense, workaholic existence." In these cases, the individuals were often facing more than just a disruption in their work lives but also a dramatic change in their personal lives.

Others gave names that put a positive spin on their experiences: "Emancipation of the slave"; "The great leap of faith"; "Working in a way that is meaningful again." In these cases, the planning and start of the change brought a great sense of relief and calm.

When naming a transition after it is over, a retrospective look includes recalling the emotional and personal experience it was. Some names brought back fond memories or labelled the difficulties these transitions brought with them. For some,

naming became the means of celebrating what they were able to do during their transitions. The name reflected either the level of distress they experienced during the transition (the negative names) or a renewed personal hope when the transition had a positive impact.

As you think about the name for your transition, keep in mind you will need to answer: "How long?" "How?" and "Why"?

Answering the question "How long?"

Knowing the actual time frame for your transition before you begin it is difficult. The ending is often a complete unknown. Sometimes it is possible to predict how long it may take, if you have figured out your ideal way for it to end.

Don't worry about precise predictions of how long, because you are the only one who will remember the target you've set. The answer to this question should be a sentence that sums up your feeling that you have begun a new path or passed the period of uncertainty.

Here are some examples of statements showing that you want to be purposeful about the benefit of taking time for the transition:

- "The transition will allow me the time to rebuild my energy and enthusiasm."
- "The transition will give me time to learn the new techniques and skills I need to move on to a new career."
- "I want to make this a period of time I will recall with pride."

Here is a statement that indicates your budget will set the time limit for your transition.

- "I have set aside money for my transition to cover all the costs of my training course and my travel."

The budget you set will define the length of time you can spend on any new activities or routines. If you have no new

source of income or have a declining income, the time period will be finite. Also, if you ask for financial support from friends and family to invest in your own personal development, you will want to be able to repay that money quickly after the transition is over.

For work transitions, your budget could include the cost of travel to explore work opportunities in other cities or countries. You might also want to invest in a business, which would bring a new type of work activity or lifestyle change you want or need.

As you start to invest in your life or work transition by spending time or money, you will be able to measure these in a very concrete way. They might be the key markers of your progress.

Answering the question "How?"

Your answer to the question of how you will spend your time is the most important part of your announcement. Your statement can serve as a message of self-confidence and certainty.

Most transitions do not have a logical sequence of steps that allow simple explanations. If you have already had the experience of a transition, you may want to compare it to your current experience.

- "My last transition started very slowly, and then, after three months, it felt like I was on a new platform and I saw my life from a new perspective."

You may want to ask for the support of close friends and family.

- "I think I will need your support along the way. May I check in with you every few weeks and tell you what has been happening?"

You also may want to highlight your action plan.

- "One of the things that will keep me energized is my

weekly logging of what has happened. I am going to try to monitor the progress of my plan."

- "I want to enjoy a completely open timetable for my transition. This open-ended flow makes me feel I can be spontaneous about every twist and turn".

Answering the question "Why?"

Here are some examples from interviews.

In terms of work:

—taking early retirement from a corporation.

After taking early retirement and spending time to consider what she could continue to do in another workplace, Esther began a new job that supported a more balanced life. She got a great boost of confidence at the farewell retirement party held for her after a 26-year career with one organization. The outpouring of recognition she received from colleagues thrilled her. "Every exit through one door leads to another door opening—a new opportunity and new experience."

—working full-time to boost confidence.

Rachel accepted an offer to join an organization as a full-time employee, after having done contract work for them for many years. The only downside was getting up at the same time every morning. The benefit of the transition was having the confidence to say she is worth more. "I had always seemed confident but underneath was questioning myself. This new role has given me a new kind of confidence."

—changing your environment.

Karl went to university to take his MSc. so that he would have more job choices. He got a job working with a small team of researchers, fulfilling his long-time dream of having colleagues who appreciated him and his contribution to the team.

In terms of life:

—being more true to yourself.

"I am focusing more on developing my creative side." After having been away for five years, Rita decided to return to the city where she had begun her career. The move back was disruptive with the challenges of rebuilding her work life. One of her important lessons was "learning that my head and my heart have to meet" in order to feel she is living her life being true to herself.

—changing work to reconnect to emotional/philosophical roots.

Stan started his transition at the age of 30, when he was questioning his own work-life situation. He found that the greatest influence on a new approach to his work was his "ability to reconnect to his family's roots and their values." By this he meant that he felt some urgency to understand and return to the values of his grandparents and their philosophical approach to life. This allowed him to "shake some of the outside influences" that made him conform to what others in his work situation expected of him. In his view, this was holding him back. The support he gained from people who helped him reconnect to his roots was key to his benefiting from his transition. He is now working as a musician within a new work setting. He feels he can be creative and authentic in a new and profound way.

These transitionees left the period of their transition feeling both nostalgic and liberated. They found these experiences were catalysts for renewal and rebuilding during the next phase.

How positive psychology and the science of emotions and health explain transitions

No discussion of work or life transitions today would be complete without the frame of reference that the movement of positive psychology offers. It affirms the importance of helping people face difficulties by building on the strengths they have. The movement also credits the support of people

who will encourage and accept whatever path a transitionee chooses.

Martin E. P. Seligman, a former president of the American Psychological Association, is one of the founders of the positive psychology movement. His research on children, set out in his book *Learned Optimism* (1991), helped him to build his new ideas. His seminal book *Authentic Happiness* (2002) facilitated the growth of this new orientation toward an understanding of human behaviour. He is currently promoting positive psychology as the way of the future for practitioners of psychology. In a recent collection of edited articles (**Keyes and Haidt, editors**) entitled *Flourishing: Positive Psychology and the Life Well Lived* (2003), Seligman's foreword emphasizes that the human condition has a naturally positive orientation to living. More specifically, he states, "The positive emotions of confidence, hope, and trust, for example, serve us best not when life is easy but when life is difficult" (Foreword, xii). The book presents a case for looking at life experience as a foundation for building on the strengths of individuals confronting unexpected barriers or setbacks.

Esther Sternberg is a physician whose scientific career has focused on the link between emotions and health. In her book entitled *The Balance Within: The Science Connecting Health and Emotions* (2001), she provides a comprehensive review of the research to date. This book became a personal story after she experienced the benefits of a sabbatical on the island of Crete while completing the manuscript. She had a complete recovery from arthritis and thyroiditis. She talked about her remarkable transition, or transformation, in an interview for an article about her work by Mark Witten in *Saturday Night* (March 2004). Here is what she explained: "When I got there, I could barely walk because of arthritis. I did not want to do a lot of exercise.... It was the most idyllic experience. I swam in the Mediterranean and walked a little

more each day. By the end of the trip, I was hiking around the hills. You could argue that it took a few months for the thyroid hormone to kick in, but that experience really opened my mind to the concept that believing can make you well. It was like a miracle. I came back healed."

In her book, Sternberg concludes the chapter "Connecting to Others" by defining emotional connections as keys to our being. She emphasizes the positive impact of an individual's "social world on health" (p. 157). These words offer another point of view on the benefit of the support of trusted and caring people during transitions. The following quote captures this sentiment powerfully: "Too little interaction – loneliness – and we can wither; too much negative social interaction, and our stress response goes into overdrive. But a rich and varied fabric of positive relationships can be the strongest net to save us in our times of deepest need" (p. 157).

Building a concrete record of your transition

Every transition has so many peaks and valleys that keeping track with a log or journal is an ideal way to remember it all. The log can also be a source of ideas for any future transitions, as there will be lessons learned from both the adventure and the challenges.

Sometimes there are experiences during a transition that will create new understanding of yourself and how change affects you. For example, your family and friends may comment that you are looking less frantic. As you develop your chronological log, you could include photographs of yourself. Tracking the progress you are making and how you think you are doing is a valuable tool, but only if you enjoy doing it – do not make it a chore.

Here are the questions that will prompt your thinking before you start to tell people about your plan for a transition.

Phase III: Five ways to tell people about your transition plan

1. Career/life patterns: work/play
   - What will you call your transition?
   - Do you have a name for it?
2. Relationships
   - Whom will you spend time with on a regular basis (friends or confidants)?
3. Vision/goals: What will the future look like?
   - How will you describe the purpose of your transition?
4. Self-awareness: Who am I?
   - How will you explain what is most important to preserve in your work or life after the transition?
5. The kind of transition experience
   - What is the strategy (how will you spend the time you have set aside) for your transition?
   - How long do you think it will last?

Phase IV: Building new routines and new prospects for work or life

In order to make your transition a building block for the next work or life period, you may want to think about what you are interested in changing in your daily routines. The courage of your mind will be a catalyst for this kind of shift. Making the transition work for you is one way of looking at it as a time for review and recasting your routines. Use it to prepare for what your life and work routines will look like when you are at the end of your transition. To quote Dennis, whom I interviewed about his recent planned transition, "Transitions are the opportunity to flex the muscle that is your personality so it remains flexible and resilient."

Many of those who planned their transitions revealed they had profound experiences. Most said they were very happy they made the decision to plan a work or life transition.

Your first transition: What did you do to make it happen? What made it memorable?

You might want to think about the first transition you ever made. For most people, it was when they left their parents' home to set out on their own. Some set up a household with friends or lived in a student residence. Others lived independently. Some people started working full-time, some continued to study in a post-secondary educational program, and others travelled.

Baby-boomers in Canada saw leaving home as an initiation rite. These departures were not always smooth. In the '60s, there were many who fled their parents to take up life in a new way. These were often stormy departures, prompted by a new culture of protest and dropping out of society as it was reshaping. No matter whether the departure was planned or spontaneous, the experience of having to count on friends, as opposed to parents, was a transition.

Try to remember the feeling you had when you first left home. It might have included exhilaration at your newfound freedom and the wide horizon of possibilities, as well as fear of the unknown. Can you imagine yourself at this crossroads again? Whenever there is an opportunity to plan a work or life transition, make sure you are as ambitious as you were when you left home for the first time. If you cannot recall that crossroads vividly, there may have been other transitions with lessons you learned. What were some of the lessons?

Here are the types of lessons I have heard people recall:
Lessons learned about how I like to live:

- I am a morning person and can start my day with energy and joy.
- I need time to get myself ready for the day, especially if I have not had my coffee.
- I am a night owl and enjoy the peace of the night hours to myself. I don't want to have to turn off the lights before

midnight.

Lessons about the type of people I can live or work with best:

- I am not the "life of the party" kind of person. But I like to work with people who will inspire me with their off-the-wall ideas and antics.
- I'll work with anyone who has a good sense of humour.
- Let me work with people who respect my privacy. I need my space, and I prefer to be left alone to do my own thing.
- Don't make me work as part of a "rah-rah" team. You won't get my buy-in. Either I take charge or I do it on my own.

Lessons about how I spend my time away from work:

- I like to be able to get out of the city I work in so weekends are a real break.
- I prefer a job that can be left on Friday and returned to on Monday.
- I need to be able to do my daily exercise routines.
- Movies are part of my weekly entertainment.
- Hearing my favourite jazz band/orchestra once in a while is essential to my keeping sane. Singing in a choir makes my life more peaceful.
- Let me get out onto the pavement for my daily run and I can face anything at work.

Starting a new transition

Whatever you choose to do after the transition is over should not influence how you spend the early part of your transition. Perhaps you can take time to get back to some hobbies you had to drop years ago—this is the time to see whether they still are important to you. The beginning of your transition will offer you time to review where you are. One woman described the beginning of her transition as seeing her life in freeze frames. It felt like everything was in slow motion. She liked this shift from the high-pressure, frantic pace of life before her transition began. It allowed her to take stock and review her priorities.

What do you think you might want to do at the start of your transition, aside from planning your next steps?

There are many ways to answer that question. Some transitionees described the early period of their transitions as time for:

- taking a break from working full-time to build some new, work-related skills;
- moving back to their home city;
- moving to a new location where they would be nearer to family;
- reorganizing their work life so it allowed more flexibility and time for special outside interests; and
- spending more time with family and friends to rebuild relationships.

Among the range of options for you, are you using the transition to help you begin to change the routines in your life? For example, if you made a list of your weekly activities, did you leave some open spaces in your calendar for some new activities? Or, once you have made your list, cross out one or two activities that you would like to replace with something else. Try the change for a few weeks. Ask friends and family for feedback about what they have noticed about you after you have made these changes. You may decide these changes in your routines should become permanent.

Whether your life or work changes after the transition, the transition period builds the bridge to a solid and clean launch for the change. When change is incremental, it may be integrated into your work or life situation gradually. However, if you are planning a change that has a specific start date, you will want to build the energy and life rhythm for that start date over time. That is one way of using the transition. It readies you for the shift and the end of the transition.

Many people who plan transitions find it convenient to set an actual date for their crossroads. If you can be as deliberate

as that, then try to be ready for this shift so the crossroads feels seamless. One transitionee described her move to a new work situation as giving her "the freedom to throw myself into unfamiliar circumstances and the ability to goof bravely." She admitted the transition helped her to empathize more with people who are in horrible workplaces and want to leave. She will never allow a repeat of that scenario at work.

Here are the questions that will prompt your thinking as you consider new routines and activities during your transition.

Phase IV: Five ways to build new routines and new prospects for work or life

1. Career/life patterns: work/play
   • Do any of the lessons you learned from past transitions apply to the current transition? What were they?

2. Relationships
   • Who will continue to be important to you both during and after transition?
   • Which people will become part of your inner circle after the transition?

3. Vision/goals: What will the future look like?
   • Are there any elements of the transition experience you will keep for (will build into) the next phase of your life?

4. Self-awareness: Who am I?
   • How will you measure the benefits of the changes introduced during the transition?

5. The kind of transition experience
   • What activities should you practice regularly during your transition?
   • Which activities will become routine?

PART TWO

On the next page is a summary chart for Part Two.

In the appendix, page 140 you can find worksheets and related questions for each of the four phases. These worksheets are offered as reminder of the kinds of questions that will help you build your planned transition skill set and your courage of the mind.

SUMMARY CHART
Choosing to plan life-enhancing transitions

How do I build courage of the mind?	I. Deciding to make a work or life change	II. Defining your transition experience	III. Telling people about your transition plan	IV. Building new routines and new prospects for work or life
1. Career and life patterns: work and play	Have you experienced work or life transitions before? If yes, what do you remember?	Which activities from either your work or play do you want to preserve—or eliminate—during your transition?	What will you call your transition? Do you have a name for it?	Do any of the lessons you learned from past transitions apply to the current transition? What were they?
2. Relationships	Who among your friends and family will support you through the transition?	Whom will you ask to support you or to be a catalyst for you as you begin your transition?	Whom will you spend time with on a regular basis? (i.e. friends, confidants)	Who will continue to be important to you both during and after your transition? Which people will become part of your inner circle after the transition?
3. Vision/goals: what will the future look like?	What are your dreams for the future beyond your transition?	How would you define your goals for your transition? What results are you hoping for?	How will you describe the purpose of your transition?	Are there any elements of the transition experience you will keep for/build into the next phase of your life?
4. Self-awareness: who am I?	How well do you think you know yourself? How would people who know you well describe you?	Are you an idealist or a pragmatist about what you can change?	How will you explain what is most important to preserve in your work or personal life after the transition?	How will you measure the benefits of any changes introduced during the transition?
5. The kind of transition experience	Have you ever planned or prepared for a work or life transition?	How will you keep track of your progress during your transition? Will you set a timetable?	What is the strategy—how will you spend the time you have set aside—for your transition? How long do you think it will last?	What activities should you practice doing regularly during your transition? Which activities will become routine?

CONCLUSION

CONCLUSION

In recounting the story of my unplanned health-crisis transition, I use the metaphor of being dumped on a water ski run without a towrope. This is an expression of how I felt in terms of my body losing control of the ride. However, at the end of this three-year period of work and life change, I think I underestimated how much the transition would impact my life. It was not as simple as getting out of the water and trying the ski run again.

For a start, I realized there has never been a time in my life when my age has played such a big part in influencing what happens to me. For instance, when contemplating all the work and life changes I have orchestrated or reacted to since my 20s, the idea of not being able to put in a fully active day had never once occurred to me.

Suddenly, my body lost its strength and mobility. A friend recommended I read Marni Jackson's book, *Pain: the Fifth Vital Sign* (2002). Her description of the politics of pain, as well as her overview on how pain is treated today both in traditional and alternative ways, confirmed what I had gone through myself. Each pain experience is very individual. I had learned how my mind affected my body, and how the cumulative results of distress, or anger and frustration, were key factors in undermining my body's healing resources.

Perhaps the most important thing I discovered is that a transition can help uncover who you are at the core. My health transition helped me find out not only whom I can count on, but also what will matter to me for the rest of my life.

CONCLUSION

One theme that has emerged is the convergence of my work and life. I cannot ever imagine completely retiring, as our parent's generation often did, but I now seek out activities that cross the personal and work divide. Initially, I was guided by my vision of having less pain and more mobility while gradually adding some of the work I had had to stop doing a few years ago. I discovered that some of my work was no longer as important to me or brought me the same kind of joy or fulfillment as it once did. However, I now have a new appreciation for the benefits of integrating my work with my needs and desires in my personal life.

The important measure of whether an activity matters is its *sustainability*. Transitions allow ongoing experimentation and testing of new and different ways of living and working. Through trial and error, some activities will be added and others dropped. The sustainable ones are those that continue to bring meaning and purpose to how you live and work. With each transition comes an interlude where the privilege of continuing the exploration of what matters in work and life is possible.

I now feel my life will likely be more packed with transitions than ever before. After all, research shows that we are all living longer and staying healthier. If most of us choose to remain actively engaged in our work through our 70s—which many people from previous generations have done, working at what they have built or created—then we will all be learning these transition skills. As one of my interviewees put it, "You can get as much out of life as you want if you master these skills— but it may be a very different life."

Personally, I hope I can continue to live and work in a new kind of combination that will be sustainable for another 10 years. I am not sure what that means in concrete terms, but I do know one thing: every new transition will leave me a precious legacy to use in preparing for the next.

APPENDIX

APPENDIX

PART ONE
COURAGE OF THE HEART

Worksheets

Dealing with unplanned life-altering transitions

How do I build courage of the heart?	Accepting the emotional impact of an unexpected work or life event
1. Talk to people whom you trust	What are the unknowns?
	What do I no longer have?
	What do I miss?

	What are the knowns?
2. Commit to regular activities providing relief	What do I still have?
	What do I cherish and will do more of?
3. Create your own transition story	When/what was my defining moment?
	What were the signs/signals that this was going to happen?

4. Find guides to help you navigate your transition	How do I find out how I am doing?
	How do I check my physical, mental and emotional health?
5. Learn about what you need to heal your heart	Whom can I talk to with experience of this kind of life-altering transition?
	How have others moved beyond their transitions?

How do I build courage of the heart?	Getting the support you need to rebuild your confidence
1. Talk to people whom you trust	Who is there for me now, and who is not?
2. Commit to regular activities providing relief	Which activities give me a boost now?
3. Create your own transition story	How do I explain what I am doing now?
	What should I call it?
	What is this chapter in my life?

	How do I rebuild my faith in myself?
4. *Find guides to help you navigate your transition*	
	How do I spend my free time?
5. *Learn about what you need to heal your heart*	What are the main barriers I am facing while moving through this transition?

How do I build courage of the heart?	Building new routines as you explore new options
1. Talk to people whom you trust	Who can I count on to give me feedback on my progress?
	How do I ask for feedback?
2. Commit to regular activities providing relief	How do I build these activities into my life?
	What can I be sure of continuing to do?

3. *Create your own transition story*	How do I explain the benefits of these new routines?
4. *Find guides to help you navigate your transition*	Which routines will support my moving beyond this transition?
5. *Learn about what you need to heal your heart*	How will I know when I am ready to move beyond the transition?

How do I build courage of the heart?	Giving back to people who have helped you
1. Talk to people whom you trust	How do I reciprocate to the people who have helped me?
2. Commit to regular activities providing relief	How do I give back to myself and to others?
	How can I be better prepared for the next transition?

3. Create your own transition story	How have I benefited from this transition?
	What have I compromised through this transition?
4. Find guides to help you navigate your transition	Who will help me sustain my healed heart?
5. Learn about what you need to heal your heart	What lessons did I learn that help guide what I do next?

How do I build courage of the heart?	Finding meaning in your transition and moving on
1. Talk to people whom you trust	How should I express pride in my courage of the heart?
2. Commit to regular activities providing relief	What do I add to my work or personal-life activities to demonstrate what I want and hope for?
3. Create your own transition story	How do I explain how my transition ended and how it led to a new beginning?

4. *Find guides to help you navigate your transition*	How do new guides help me move through and beyond my transition?
5. *Learn about what you need to heal your heart*	How do I demonstrate that I have moved on from my transition?
	What actions are key reminders of the courage of my heart?

APPENDIX

PART TWO
COURAGE OF THE MIND

Worksheets

Choosing to plan life-enhancing transitions

How do I build courage of the mind?	Deciding to make a work or life change.
1. Career and life patterns: work and play	Have you experienced work or life transitions before? If so, what do you remember?
2. Relationships	Who among your friends and family will support you through the transition?

3. *Vision/goals: what will the future look like?*	What are your dreams for the future, beyond your transition?
4. *Self-awareness: who am I?*	How well do you think you know yourself?
	How would people who know you well describe you?
5. *The kind of transition experience*	Have you ever planned or prepared for a work or life transition?

How do I build courage of the mind?	Defining your transition experience
1. Career and life patterns: work and play	Which activities from either your work or play do you want to preserve—or eliminate—during your transition?
2. Relationships	Whom will you ask to support you, or to be a catalyst for you, as you begin your transition?
3. Vision/goals: what will the future look like?	How would you define your goals for your transition?
	What results are you hoping for?

4. *Self-awareness: who am I?*	Are you an idealist or a pragmatist about what you can change?
5. *The kind of transition experience*	How will you keep track of your progress during your transition?
	Will you set a timetable?

How do I build courage of the mind?	Telling people about your transition plan
1. Career and life patterns: work and play	What will you call your transition?
	Do you have a name for it?
2. Relationships	Whom will you spend time with on a regular basis? (i.e. friends, confidants)
3. Vision/goals: what will the future look like?	How will you describe the purpose of your transition?

4. *Self-awareness: who am I?*	Are you an idealist or a pragmatist about what you can change?
5. *The kind of transition experience*	What is the strategy—how will you spend the time you have set aside—for your transition?
	How long do you think it will last?

How do I build courage of the mind?	Building new routines and new prospects for work or life
1. Career and life patterns: work and play	Do any of the lessons you learned from past transitions apply to the current transition? What were they?
2. Relationships	Who will continue to be important to you both during and after your transition?
	Which people will become part of your inner circle after the transition?

3. *Vision/goals: what will the future look like?*	Are there any elements of the transition experience that you will keep for/build into the next phase of your life?
4. *Self-awareness: who am I?*	How will you measure the benefits of any changes introduced during the transition?
5. *The kind of transition experience*	What activities should you practice doing regularly during your transition?
	Which activities will become routine?

PART TWO
COURAGE OF THE MIND

Questions to ask yourself before planning a transition

1. The transition I am facing is								
Self-directed/planned	1	2	3	4	5	6	7	Unexpected/ unplanned
2. How much stress do you think you will experience when the transition starts?								
Little stress	1	2	3	4	5	6	7	Very stressful
3.a. How significant an impact do you think the transition will have on your work situation?								
Not dramatic/ significant	1	2	3	4	5	6	7	Very dramatic/ significant
3.b How significant an impact do you think the transition will have on your personal life situation?								
Not dramatic/ significant	1	2	3	4	5	6	7	Very dramatic/ significant
4.a How long do you think it will take, or how long are you prepared to let it take, until you feel you are on a new path in terms of your *work situation?*								
Very little time	1	2	3	4	5	6	7	A lot of time
4.b How long do you think it will take, or how long are you prepared to let it take, until you feel you are on a new path in terms of your *personal life situation?*								
Very little time	1	2	3	4	5	6	7	A lot of time
5. How much preparation do you think you need before you start your transition?								
Little preparation	1	2	3	4	5	6	7	Lots of preparation
6. Do you expect the experience will lead to significant lessons you will learn about yourself?								
No lessons	1	2	3	4	5	6	7	Significant lessons
7. How much change to your life are you willing to have because of the transition?								
No change to my life	1	2	3	4	5	6	7	Lots of change to my life

Transition Score Chart

1.	Self-directed/ planned	1	2	3	4	5	6	7	Unexpected/ unplanned
2.	Little stress	1	2	3	4	5	6	7	Very stressful
3.a	Not dramatic/significant impact on personal life	1	2	3	4	5	6	7	Very dramatic/ significant Impact on personal life
3.b	Not dramatic/significant impact on work life	1	2	3	4	5	6	7	Very dramatic/ significant impact on work life
4.a	Three months to new path in personal life	1	2	3	4	5	6	7	Three years to new path in personal life
4.b	Three months to new path in work life	1	2	3	4	5	6	7	Three years to new path in work life
5.	Little preparation	1	2	3	4	5	6	7	Lots of preparation
6.	No lessons	1	2	3	4	5	6	7	Significant lessons
7.	No change to life	1	2	3	4	5	6	7	Lots of change to life
Total									
Overall Total									

Scoring

Transpose the circled numbers from the Questions Chart and calculate the overall total. Total up all the columns at the bottom of the chart. Your final overall total will range from a low of 9 (which will mean that you circled all the "1"'s in the first column), to a total of "63" (which will mean you have circled all "7"s). The higher your overall total, the more support you are likely to need to facilitate your transition.

PART TWO
COURAGE OF THE MIND
People supports and where to find them

WHAT I NEED	WHY	POSSIBLE SOURCE
Appreciation	I haven't got the recognition I deserve.	Spouse or partner, friends, mentor, career coach, faith community, ethno-cultural community.
Emotional and psychological support	I feel scared and/or alone. I need the warmth and caring of an intimate confidante.	Spouse or partner, older children, mentor, friends, career coach, support group.
	I am living my life in ways that are harmful to me or others	Psychologist, social worker, psychotherapist, psychiatrist.
Financial support	My income is going to go down while, or if, I make the transition.	Partner, spouse, family member, financial institution.
Healthier life-style	I am not taking care of my health. I have some chronic health problems.	Physician, naturopath, holistic nutritionist, personal-fitness trainer, homeopathic health practitioner, yoga or pilates teacher.
Non-Judge-mental advice	I don't want to be driven by someone else's agenda.	People who listen to me and do not evaluate my ideas.
Objective sounding board	I'm too close to the issues to know if I'm deluding myself or missing something important.	People who I can trust to be honest and direct, and listen and reflect back to me what my ideas sound like to them.
Reality check	I'm wondering if I'm off-base in how I'm seeing things or in what I am planning to do.	People who will be able to understand what obstacles I might face and also how my ideas will help me get to where I want to go.
Reassurance	I **am** doing the right thing.	People who will support my decision and give me encouragement as I move forward.

INTERVIEW QUESTIONS

Respondents were baby-boomers born between 1946 and 1966

Introduction

The purpose of this confidential interview is to ask you about your most *recent personal experience of a unique change in your life or work*, which you might call an important transition or crossroads. Please consider the experience from the point of view of how you would tell the story.

All interviews will take place face-to-face. However, I believe you may be more comfortable seeing the questions in advance. The questions you will be asked in the interview, therefore, are reproduced below.

Your answers to the questions will, hopefully, help to describe the lessons you learned about yourself and what you would recommend to others who face a similar transitional crossroads.

All interviews will be aggregated and general themes will become the framework for my upcoming book. Some questions include a rating scale on which you can quantify your experience.

Question 1

a) Please describe the most memorable transition or crossroads you faced recently (e.g., work, your life circumstance, your lifestyle).

b) How did this most recent transition start? Did you make a decision to begin, or was there a defining moment which prompted it?

c) On a scale from 1 to 7, how planned or unplanned was it?

Question 2

a) If you were to compare this recent transition to other life/work transition experiences, were they the same or different in terms of what prompted or preceded them?
- What were some similarities?
- What were some differences?

b) Did any *pattern* you understood from previous transition/ crossroads experiences influence how you handled your most recent experience, and, if so, in what way?

Question 3

a) How did you feel during the early stages of the transition/ crossroads?

b) How much stress did you experience when you faced this transition/crossroads? (You will be asked to rate on a scale from 1 to 7.)

c) What form did that stress take?

Question 4

a) If you felt there was significant disruption during the transition, can you describe what that was like? How did you deal with it?

b) How dramatic/significant was the crossroads to your work? (You will be asked to rate on a scale from 1 to 7.)

b) How dramatic/significant was the crossroads to your personal life situation (health, relationships, routines, other)? (You will be asked to rate on a scale from 1 to 7.)

Question 5

a) What was the biggest barrier you faced in moving through the transition?

b) What was the biggest boost that helped you move beyond the crossroads?

c) How long did it take you to go beyond the transition/cross-

roads to what felt like a new direction or a new platform or new path for yourself in your work?

d) In your personal-life situation?

Question 6

a) What did you do to prepare yourself for the recent crossroads?

b) Please rate how emotionally ready you were for this experience. (You will be asked to rate on a scale from 1 to 7.)

c) Please rate how prepared you were in terms of such concrete measures as financial resources, tactical steps to take and the physical effort required. (You will be asked to rate on a scale from 1 to 7.)

d) If you were *not* ready or prepared to deal with the transition/crossroads, what did you do to try to get ready or be better prepared ?

Question 7

a) Did you feel you needed any support to deal with/make the transition? (If not, skip to 7f.)

b) If yes, what kinds of support did you think you needed (e.g. people, things, circumstances)?

c) Were you able to get the support you needed? (If not, skip to 7f.)

d) If you did draw on support, please describe the nature of that support and what you valued the most from it.

e) What would you recommend to others about what to look for in people who provide support during transitions?

f) If you didn't feel you needed any support, what impact did that have on your ability to make the transition happen?

Question 8

a) Through the evolution of your most recent transition/crossroads experience, were there benefits and upsides? (You will be asked to rate on a scale from 1 to 7.)

b) If there were significant benefits/upsides, what were they?

c) What about negatives or downsides? (You will be asked to rate on a scale from 1 to 7.)

d) If there were significant negatives and downsides, how would you describe them?

Question 9

a) Looking back on the result of your most recent transition experience, did it meet your expectations? Why/why not?

b) Looking back on your most recent crossroads experience, is there anything you would have done differently?

c) the transition has ended, would you consider it ended well or not well? (You will be asked to rate on a scale from 1 to 7.)

Question 10

a) Were there lessons you learned about yourself from your most recent crossroads/transition experience that will help you in the next transition? (You will be asked to rate on a scale from 1 to 7.)

b) If lessons were significant, what were they?

Question 11

a) At some point, did you say, "I know I made the right decision" or "I am glad this happened to me"?

b) At some point, did you say, "I know I made the wrong decision" or "I am sorry this happened to me"?

c) If you said "yes" to 11a or 11b, please describe what it was like: how did you feel?

Question 12

a) Have you tried to help others with their own transition/crossroads experiences?

b) If so, could you provide an example?

Question 13

How are you living your life differently now, as a result of the transition/crossroads experience you had recently?

Question 14

If there was only one thing you could tell people about this transition/crossroads experience, what would it be?

DEMOGRAPHIC QUESTIONS

D1   Date of birth (y/m/d) _____/_____/____

D2   Birthplace_____

D3   Gender   M / F

D4   Post-secondary education_____

D5   Current job: please check off a category from list below:

   1_____business professional in firm/corporation
   2_____self-employed
   3_____management
   4_____technical/sales
   5_____mental and physical health care
   6_____the arts and culture
   7_____administrative/clerical
   8_____other (specify)

D6   First language (mother tongue)_____

D7a Year started working full time_____

D7b Did you begin full-time work and independent living simultaneously? If so, when?

D8   Did you begin full-time work and live in a communal arrangement with shared responsibilities? If so, when?

D9   Did you have any gaps in your work life that were more than one year? If so, when?

D10 How would you rate the importance of your work life to your overall life experience on a scale from 1 to 7, with 1 meaning "I work to allow me to earn enough to live" and 7 meaning "My work defines my life."

DATA TABLES

**Tabulated answers to
some of the questions on the questionnaire**

**Question 3B
How much stress did you experience
when you faced this transition?**

Transition experience	Total respondents (N)=75	Level of stress		
		Little 1-3	4-5	A Lot 6-7
Planned	47	34%	26%	40%
Unplanned	28	18%	15%	68%

Age groups	Total respondents (N)=75	Level of stress		
		Little 1-3	4-5	A Lot 6-7
38-47	21	34%	20%	48%
48-52	23	34%	17%	47%
53+	31	19%	25%	54%

Gender	Total respondents (N)=75	Level of stress		
		Little 1-3	4-5	A Lot 6-7
Male	34	21%	18%	61%
Female	41	34%	24%	41%

Question 5C

How long did it take you to go beyond the transition to what felt like a new direction or new path for yourself in your work?

Transition experience	Total Respondents (N)=75	From largest percentage					
		6 mos	1 year	3 mos	2 years	18 mos	3 years*
Planned	47	15%	13%	11%	9%	9%	6%
Unplanned	28	25%	14%	14%	14%	11%	7%

Age group	Total Respondents (N)=75	From largest percentage					
		6 mos	1 year	3 mos	2 years	18 mos	3 years
38-47	21	19%	14%	10%	10%	5%	5%
48-52	23	22%	13%	4%	9%	17%	13%
53+	31	16%	13%	19%	13%	6%	3%

Gender	Total respondents (N)=75	From largest percentage					
		6 mos	1 year	3 mos	2 years	18 mos	3 years
Male	34	6%	12%	15%	12%	15%	9%
Female	41	29%	15%	10%	10%	5%	5%

★ Very few people experienced other time frames.

Question 5D

How long did it take you to go beyond the transition to what felt like a new direction or new path for yourself in your personal life?

Transition experience	Total respondents (N)=75	From largest percentage					
		1 year	6 mos	3 years	2 mos	2 years	Instant*
Planned	47	11%	17%	9%	6%	9%	6%
Unplanned	28	29%	11%	11%	7%	4%	7%

Age groups	Total respondents (N)=75	From largest percentage					
		1 year	6 mos	3 years	2 mos	2 years	immediate
38-47	21	19%	5%	5%	10%	10%	10%
48-52	23	22%	22%	13%	9%	4%	13%
53+	31	13%	16%	10%	3%	6%	0%

Gender	Total respondents (N)=75	From largest percentage					
		1 year	6 mos	3 years	2 mos	2 years	immediate
Male	34	21%	12%	15%	3%	6%	6%
Female	41	15%	17%	5%	10%	7%	7%

* Very few people experienced other time frames.

Question 6B

How emotionally ready were you for your transition?

Transition experience	Total respondents (N)=75	Degree of readiness		
		Very ready 1-3	4-5	Not ready at all 6-7
Planned	47	68%	20%	13%
Unplanned	28	43%	25%	32%

Age groups	Total respondents (N)=75	Degree of readiness		
		Very ready 1-3	4-5	Not ready at all 6-7
38-47	21	62%	20%	19%
48-52	23	74%	13%	13%
53+	31	45%	29%	25%

Gender	Total respondents (N)=75	Degree of readiness		
		Very ready 1-3	4-5	Not ready at all 6-7
Male	34	59%	18%	24%
Female	41	58%	24%	17%

Question 6C

How tactically prepared—e.g. financially, physically— were you for your transition?

Transition experience	Total respondents (N)=75	Degree of preparedness		
		Very prepared 1-3	4-5	Not prepared at all 6-7
Planned	47	77%	20%	4%
Unplanned	28	65%	11%	25%

Age groups	Total respondents (N)=75	Degree of preparedness		
		Very prepared 1-3	4-5	Not prepared at all 6-7
38-47	21	67%	29%	5%
48-52	23	81%	8%	8%
53+	31	68%	12%	19%

Gender	Total respondents (N)=75	Degree of preparedness		
		Very prepared 1-3	4-5	Not prepared at all 6-7
Male	34	60%	24%	18%
Female	41	83%	10%	7%

Questions 7A and 9A

Did you feel you needed any support to deal with the transition?

Looking back on the results, were your expectations met?

Transition experience	Total respondents (N)=75	#7A: Support?			#9A: Transition met expectations?		
		Yes	No	Both	Yes	No	No expec- tations
Planned	47	91%	6%	2%	91%	6%	2%
Unplanned	28	93%	7%	0%	79%	7%	14%

Age groups	Total respondents (N)=75	#7A: Support ?			#9A: Transition met expectations?		
		Yes	No	Both	Yes	No	No expec- tations
38-47	21	95%	5%	0%	81%	10%	10%
48-52	23	87%	9%	4%	91%	4%	4%
53+	31	94%	6%	0%	87%	6%	6%

Gender	Total respondents (N)=75	#7A: Support?			#9A: Transition met expectations?		
		Yes	No	Both	Yes	No	No expec- tations
Male	34	91%	9%	0%	85%	9%	6%
Female	41	93%	5%	2%	88%	5%	7%

Question 8A

Were there benefits and upsides to your transition?

Transition experience	Total respondents (N)=75	Degree of benefits		
		Little 1-3	4-5	A lot 6-7
Planned	47	0%	20%	81%
Unplanned	28	4%	32%	65%

Age groups	Total respondents (N)=75	Degree of benefits		
		Little 1-3	4-5	A lot 6-7
38-47	21	0%	19%	81%
48-52	23	4%	17%	78%
53+	31	0%	32%	67%

Gender	Total respondents (N)=75	Degree of benefits		
		Little 1-3	4-5	A lot 6-7
Male	34	0%	24%	76%
Female	41	2%	24%	73%

Question 8C

Were there negatives and downsides to your transition?

Transition experience	Total respondents (N)=75	Degree of negatives		
		Little 1-3	4-5	A lot 6-7
Planned	47	70%	19%	10%
Unplanned	28	43%	32%	25%

Age groups	Total respondents (N)=75	Degree of negatives		
		Little 1-3	4-5	A lot 6-7
38-47	21	72%	15%	15%
48-52	23	48%	30%	22%
53+	31	61%	26%	13%

Gender	Total respondents (N)=75	Degree of negatives		
		Little 1-3	4-5	A lot 6-7
Male	34	62%	27%	12%
Female	41	58%	22%	19%

Question 11

Do you feel you made the right decision or the wrong decision?

Transition experience	Total respondents (N)=75	Know made right decision	Glad happened to me	Both made right decision and glad happened	Sorry it happened	Both glad and sorry it happened	Best professional experience had
Total	75	67%	27%	3%	1%	1%	1%
Planned	47	79%	17%	2%	0%	0%	2%
Unplanned	28	46%	43%	4%	4%	4%	0%

Age groups	Total respondents (N)=75	Know made right decision	Glad happened to me	Both made right decision and glad happened	Sorry it happened	Both glad and sorry it happened	Best professional experience had
38-47	21	62%	24%	5%	0%	5%	5%
48-52	23	83%	17%	0%	0%	0%	0%
53+	31	58%	35%	3%	3%	0%	0%

Gender	Total respondents (N)=75	Know made right decision	Glad happened to me	Both made right decision and glad happened	Sorry it happened	Both glad and sorry it happened	Best professional experience had
Male	34	56%	35%	6%	3%	0%	0%
Female	41	76%	20%	0%	0%	2%	2%

Questions 12A and 13

Percentages for yes/no (concluding questions)

Transition experience	Total respondents (N)=75	Total respondents (%)	#12A: Help others with their transitions		#13: Living life differently		
			Yes	No	Yes	No	Both
Planned	47	63%	89%	11%	89%	9%	2%
Unplanned	28	37%	93%	7%	96%	0%	4%

Age groups	Total respondents (N)=75	Total respondents (%)	#12A: Help others with their transitions		#13: Living life differently		
			Yes	No	Yes	No	Both
38-47	21	28%	90%	10%	90%	10%	0%
48-52	23	31%	100%	0%	96%	4%	0%
53+	31	41%	84%	16%	90%	3%	6%

Gender	Total respondents (N)=75	Total respondents (%)	#12A: Help others with their transitions		#13: Living life differently		
			Yes	No	Yes	No	Both
Male	34	45%	85%	15%	91%	6%	3%
Female	41	55%	95%	5%	93%	5%	2%

Tabulated results from the demographic data questionnaire

Question D10

The importance of work life to overall life experience

Transition experience	Total respondents (N)=75	Degree of importance		
		Little 1-3	4-5	A lot 6-7
Planned	47	4%	57%	39%
Unplanned	28	25%	55%	22%

Age groups	Total respondents (N)=75	Degree of importance		
		Little 1-3	4-5	A lot 6-7
38-47	21	10%	62%	29%
48-52	23	8%	66%	26%
53+	31	16%	45%	39%

Gender	Total respondents (N)=75	Degree of importance		
		Little 1-3	4-5	A lot 6-7
Male	34	12%	42%	47%
Female	41	12%	68%	20%

Summary chart: gender

Transition experience	Total respondents (N)=75	Gender	
		Male	Female
Planned	47	43%	57%
Unplanned	28	50%	50%

Age groups	Total respondents (N)=75	Gender	
		Male	Female
38-47	21	52%	48%
48-52	23	30%	70%
53+	31	52%	48%

Gender	Total respondents (N)=75	Gender	
		Male	Female
Male	34	100%	0%
Female	41	0%	100%

BIBLIOGRAPHY

Armstrong, Lance with Sally Jenkins. *Every Second Counts*. New York, NY: Broadway Books, 2003.

Bolles, Richard N. *What Color is Your Parachute? A Practical Manual for Job-Hunters and Career-Changers*. Berkeley, CA: Ten Speed Press, 2005 (revised and updated).

Bonanno, George A. "Loss, trauma and human resilience: Have we underestimated the human capacity to thrive after extremely aversive events?" *American Psychologist*. January 2004, pp. 20-28.

Bridges, William. *Managing Transitions: Making the Most of Change*. Cambridge, Mass.: Perseus Books, 2003 (updated and expanded).

Bridges, William. *The Way of Transition: Embracing Life's Most Difficult Moments*. Cambridge, Mass.: Perseus Books, 2001.

Bridges, William. *Transitions: Making Sense of Life's Changes*. Cambridge, Mass.: Perseus Books, 1980.

Bronson, Po. *What Should I Do With My Life? The True Story of People Who Answered the Ultimate Question*. New York, NY: Random House, 2002.

Burton, Mary Lindley, and Wedemeyer, Richard A. *In Transition: From the Harvard Business School Club of New York's Career Management Seminar*. New York, NY: Harper Business, 1991.

Chopra, Deepak. *The Seven Spiritual Laws of Success: A Practical Guide to the Fulfillment of Your Dreams*. San Rafael, CA: Amber-Allen Publishing, 1994.

Dingfelder, Sadie F. "Solutions to resolution dilution." *Monitor on Psychology*. American Psychological Association, January 2004, pp. 34-36.

Dychtwald, K., Erickson, T., and Morison, B. *It's Time to Retire Retirement*. Harvard Business Review, March 2004, pp. 48-57.

Feldman, Daniel C., ed. *Work Careers: A Developmental Perspective*. San Francisco, CA: Jossey-Bass Business & Management Series, 2002.

Figler, Howard. *The Complete Job-Search Handbook: All the Skills You Need to Get Any Job and Have a Good Time Doing It*. New York, NY: Henry Holt and Co., 1988 (revised and expanded).

BIBLIOGRAPHY

Foord Kirk, Janis. *Survivability: Career Strategies for the New World of Work.* Kelowna, B.C.: Kirkfoord Communications Inc., 1999 (revised).

Foot, David K. with Daniel Stoffman. *Boom, Bust & Echo: How to Profit from the Coming Demographic Shift.* Toronto, ON: Macfarlane, Walter & Ross, 1996.

Foot, David K. with Daniel Stoffman. *Boom, Bust & Echo* 2000: *Profiting from the Demographic Shift in the New Millennium.* Toronto, ON: Macfarlane, Walter & Ross, 1998.

Freedman, Marc. *Prime Time: How Baby Boomers Will Revolutionize Retirement and Transform America.* New York, NY: Perseus Books, 1999.

Hayhurst Sr., Jim. *Where Have I Gone Right? The Right Mountain Guide to Getting the Job and Life You Want.* Toronto, ON: John Wiley & Sons Canada, Ltd., 2004.

Ibarra, Hermina. *Working Identity: Unconventional Strategies for Reinventing Your Career.* Boston, Mass.: Harvard Business School Press, 2003.

Jackson, Marni. *Pain: The Fifth Vital Sign.* Toronto, ON: Random House of Canada, 2002.

Jeffers, Susan. *Embracing Uncertainty: Breakthrough Methods for Achieving Peace of Mind When Facing the Unknown.* New York, NY: St. Martin's Griffin, 2003.

Kabat–Zinn, Jon. *Full Catastrophe Living: Using the Wisdom of Your Body and Mind to Face Stress, Pain and Illness.* New York, NY: Bantam Doubleday Dell Publishing Group, Inc., 1990.

Kabat–Zinn, Jon. *Wherever You Go, There You Are: Mindfulness Meditation in Everyday Life.* New York, NY: Hyperion, 1994.

Keyes, Corey L.M., and Haidt, Jonathan (eds.). *Flourishing: Positive Psychology and the Life Well-Lived.* Washington, D.C.: American Psychological Association, 2003.

Kubler-Ross, Elizabeth. *The Wheel of Life: A Memoir of Living and Dying.* New York, NY: Scribner (1997).

Moses, Barbara. *What Next? The Complete Guide to Taking Control of Your Working Life.* London, New York, NY: DK Publishing, Inc., 2003.

BIBLIOGRAPHY

Peck, M. Scott. *Further Along the Road Less Travelled: The Unending Journey Toward Spiritual Growth* (edited lectures). New York, NY; Toronto, ON: Simon & Shuster, 1993.

Ray, Oakley. "How the mind hurts and heals the body." *American Psychologist*, January 2004, pp. 29-40.

Salzberg, Sharon. *Loving-kindness: The Revolutionary Art of Happiness.* Boston, Mass., London: Shambhala Classics, 2002.

Salzberg, Sharon. *Faith: Trusting Your Own Deepest Experience.* New York, NY: Riverhead Books/Penguin Putnam Inc., 2002.

Seligman, Martin E.P. *Learned Optimism.* New York, NY: Knopf, 1991

Seligman, Martin E.P. *Authentic Happiness: Using the New Positive Psychology to Realize Your Potential for Lasting Fulfillment.* New York, NY: The Free Press, 2002.

Sheehy, Gail. *The Silent Passage.* Toronto, ON: Random House of Canada, 1992.

Sheehy, Gail. *New Passages: Mapping Your Life Across Time.* Toronto, ON: Random House of Canada, 1995.

Sheehy, Gail. *Understanding Men's Passages: Discovering the New Map of Men's Lives.* Toronto, ON: Random House of Canada, 1998.

Sinetar, Marsha. *Do What You Love, The Money Will Follow: Discovering Your Right Livelihood.* New York, NY: Bantam Doubleday Dell Publishing Group Inc., 1987.

Sternberg, Esther M. *The Balance Within: The Science Connecting Health and Emotions.* New York, NY: W. H. Freeman & Co., 2001.

Taylor, Daniel. *The Healing Power of Stories: Creating Yourself Through Stories of Your Life.* New York, NY: Doubleday, 1996.

Teiger, Paul D., and Barron-Tieger, Barbara. *Do What You Are: Discover the Perfect Career for You Through the Secrets of Personality Type.* New York, NY; Toronto, ON: Little Brown & Company, 1995.

Wallin, Pamela. *Speaking of Success.* Toronto, ON: Key Porter, 2001.

Witten, Mark. "Where Mind and Body Meet." *Saturday Night*, March 2004, pp. 38-43.

ACKNOWLEDGEMENTS

This creative pursuit took many paths and hit many obstacles, which I had not expected. In the beginning, I wanted to capture the guiding principles of my work as a psychologist and executive coach providing life-planning and career-planning services. It became clear, early on, that my personal life and work transitions were an important template for my book, and I decided to include some of my own transition stories.

There were many people who made it possible for me to sustain my momentum and not give up on the idea of putting my thoughts into a first book. My heartfelt thanks to them all. I would like to name a few of the people whose enthusiasm and encouragement helped me deal with some key obstacles along the way.

I am indebted to the openness and compassion Marlene Mawhinney, director of the Yoga Centre Toronto, has always shown me. At a critical juncture during the summer of 2004, I participated in Marlene's Yoga in the Heart of the City week-long workshop. At the conclusion of our week, I was sure that my framework—courage of the heart and courage of the mind—was the best one. Yoga Centre Toronto was my oasis of healing and calm as I faced lapses in confidence in writing this book.

Dr. Jennifer Bayani, chiropractor and acupuncturist, has encouraged my exploration of the link between mind and body throughout my recovery to relatively pain-free living with chronic psoriatic arthritis. As my book ideas took shape, she was a key sounding board in differentiating between planned and unplanned work and life transitions. Dr. Rachel Shupak, rheumatologist, has helped me understand my arthritic body

ACKNOWLEDGEMENTS

and what has changed permanently. She introduced me to the concept of self-efficacy, a proactive approach to living with chronic illness. Throughout my unexpected health transition, she encouraged me to seek ways of bringing myself relief, as well as believing in their sustainability. Dr. Evelyn Sommers, psychologist, encouraged me to accept my circumstance and understand how to tell my transition story as part of the book. Dr. Ester Cole, psychologist, introduced me to the concept of narrative thinking, and the emphasis on stories as one avenue for healing. This guided the types of questions I asked everyone I interviewed. During 2005, I continued to pursue alternative therapies to reduce chronic knee pain and swelling. Dr. Daria Love, naturopath, recommended new ways of promoting healing. I have benefited from all with a renewed sense of energy and a greater feeling of wellness.

I would like to thank Ann Welsh, whom I invited to participate at the birth of my research in understanding how baby-boomers experience transitions in their work or lives. We began interviewing people and clarifying the ideas as we went along. Ann, you were a delight to work with, and I do believe the project emerged better for your initial involvement. My thanks also to Meredith Renwick and Emily Polak, who helped out during different stages of the writing.

My research needed the support of data-entry and cross-tab summaries. My first choice for this support was Pollara. Early in 2001, I was welcomed into the Pollara offices as I started the period of healing from my arthritic flare-up. Everyone at Pollara, in particular Michael Marzolini and Megan McGillicuddy, made me feel very much at home at a key crossroads in my professional life. My two years in this special office environment helped me feel hopeful about the prospect of writing a first book. Since then, I have benefited from the conscientious and dependable input of Beryl Lau

ACKNOWLEDGEMENTS

and her team in the data-analysis group.

Michael Levine encouraged me to find my voice. He coached me as a newcomer to the world of publishing. I have benefited from his volleys back to me after I shared work or ideas with him.

There have been others who, in their own special way, enhanced the creative environment I needed for writing. I want to express my appreciation to Philip Somerville, our dear friend and soul mate. Philip offered his home, an oasis in Athens, Greece, as our home away from home during our summer vacations. During these breaks, the book's framework emerged. I wrote some of my key ideas and themes while on these trips. Philip was also a key editorial influence as the book was taking shape during our time together in Israel in December 2004.

During the fall of 2004, I was nurtured by the musical choices and commentary of Canada's special broadcaster, Eric Friesen. He launched his new show, *Studio Sparks*, at the same time as I began spending as many days of the week that I needed to get a first draft of my manuscript completed.

The final phase of editorial polishing and refining has been enriched by the skill and insight of Jocelyn Laurence. She facilitated my becoming a first author both in terms of what readers would want and how to get the materials ready for publication. Her colleague, Wayne Gooding, was the catalyst to finding the right title. I'd like to thank early-life friend, Ydessa Hendeles, for recommending Jocelyn and Wayne to me.

Finally, I offer a tribute to all the willing and enthusiastic transition storytellers who shared their intimate thoughts and feelings about a recent memorable work or life transition. They have enriched the experience of my recent transition immeasurably.